DESIGN YOUR *Personal Brand* PRESENCE

Valuable inputs from India's finest coaches

DIYA ASRANI

INDIA • SINGAPORE • MALAYSIA

Notion Press

No.8, 3rd Cross Street,
CIT Colony, Mylapore,
Chennai, Tamil Nadu – 600004

First Published by Notion Press 2021
Copyright © Diya Asrani 2021
All Rights Reserved.

ISBN 978-1-63781-520-5

This book has been published with all efforts taken to make the material error-free after the consent of the author. However, the author and the publisher do not assume and hereby disclaim any liability to any party for any loss, damage, or disruption caused by errors or omissions, whether such errors or omissions result from negligence, accident, or any other cause.

While every effort has been made to avoid any mistake or omission, this publication is being sold on the condition and understanding that neither the author nor the publishers or printers would be liable in any manner to any person by reason of any mistake or omission in this publication or for any action taken or omitted to be taken or advice rendered or accepted on the basis of this work. For any defect in printing or binding the publishers will be liable only to replace the defective copy by another copy of this work then available.

This book is dedicated to
my support system - My Family.

CONTENTS

Foreword 7

Preface 9

Acknowledgment 13

1. The "Aha!" Moment 15
2. The Barbed Boundary of Comfort 26
3. Moulding Your Journey 32
4. The Burning Desire 45
5. The Success Secret: Specificity 55
6. Experience + Relevance = Stories 64
7. Productivity + Progression - Perfection = Pro-Position! 71
8. Marketing Talks, Story Sells 79
9. One, Two, Three, and Action! 88
10. Design Your Presence! 96
11. Six Influence Building Myths to Bust 103

FOREWORD

This book is the golden key for every entrepreneur, coach, or trainer to building an amazing brand. Diya has beautifully explained the concept of personal branding as a tool to help one design their own presence beyond what they could possibly imagine. Her book starts with a personal experience from her childhood and subtly moves into educating the reader about the concept while also coaching them with thought-provoking questions that are simple yet so powerful in the process of building one's presence. Each chapter is an eye-opener and makes you think at every step. Whether you are starting out or are a seasoned entrepreneur or knowledge-giver, and you're looking to really understand the concept of standing out in the industry yet being your beautiful self, this book will help you move steadily towards designing your presence successfully. I personally love the way Diya coaches and trains people and have seen her create success stories on the way. This book is not just another book for you to read; it can really change the way you see success in the way you build your business in today's changing times.

If not today, then when?

PUJA PUNEET, Life Coach, author of *Unlocking The Golden Cage*, and CEO of Life By Design

Building a personal brand is not a trend but more like a necessity to thrive and grow in today's competitive business world. I always believe that human connection is what makes a business successful and what attracts people to us. Personal Branding is the need for every business owner, entrepreneur, or knowledge-giver to stand out in the industry.

And Diya's book, Design Your PERSONAL BRAND Presence, shows its importance with simplicity and generosity. Being successful doesn't stop at being great at what you do; it is also about being the solution to people's problems that makes them choose you over the others. In this book, Diya takes her reader through a thoughtful blend of her life experiences and coaching strategy that ends up with a lot of clarity around the concept of building a personal brand. As a lifestyle entrepreneur and digital coach myself, I coach and train entrepreneurs and knowledge-givers from various backgrounds; and I know how important it is to stand out in the world of digital business. This book will help you think beyond the invisible line of your comfort zone and help you move in the direction towards clarity.

Do we smell success around the corner? Definitely!

SIDDHARTH RAJSEKAR, India's leading digital coach, Lifestyle Entrepreneur

PREFACE

When the pandemic hit India in the early months of 2020, I suddenly had a lot of free time to create and build new things in my business. I had absolutely no idea about what I was going to do, but I knew that this year was going to make me do things that I had never done before or even dreamt of doing. They say the 'gut feeling' is often stronger than the feeling of love.

Little did I know that I would actually be inspired to author a book on Personal Branding, as I really wanted entrepreneurs and knowledge-givers to learn through my story how I built my own presence and launched my brand, Design Your Presence™, which got me to build a solid clientele from various parts of the world. Just like any entrepreneur starting out, I struggled to find a simplified way to create an impact. But once I did, there was no looking back!

This book has an excitingly casual and action-oriented approach towards personal branding; I want to take my readers through a process of getting more clarity about how they want to design their own presence without feeling overwhelmed or stuck.

The book has a glimpse of how I coach entrepreneurs and knowledge-givers towards building their presence. Each chapter ends with an action that they need to take as a way to gain maximum clarity in their brand-building journey.

To add some perspective, I also had the honour to interview some of the finest Indian coaches in the industry, wherein I got their insights on how one should build a presence as a leader in the industry. The leaders are carefully chosen—I have personally learned from them, and I knew that they would add value to this book.

Throughout the book, you will see snippets of the interviews, under the heading 'Interview Diaries,' done with experts like Puja Puneet, Rajiv Talreja, and Siddharth Rajsekar, wherein we cover an array of topics relevant to personal branding.

Writing this book has been a way to channelize my own personality into approaching personal branding. It took me a while to put all my stories together and build something that is personalized yet informative, but it was a fruitful journey that got me to really dive deep into how I wanted to approach it.

Having that blend in the language and tone in this book was my main goal, and I am happy to say that I managed to achieve it. They say success happens to you when you make it happen for yourself, and usually, we do a shabby job of it. The truth is I was a bit too shabby and all over the place initially, but when I finished writing this book, I realized that I could actually write, and I *actually* finished the manuscript!

A huge part of the approach toward this book has been two things:

1. My habit of journaling and 2. My hunger for learning and creating. When I started penning down my thoughts on paper, I realized, "Hey! Many people could learn from this!" I always wanted to help entrepreneurs and knowledge-givers who are so talented in what they do. And I feel that this book can be a guiding light for many looking for a casual yet actionable perspective towards building their own personal brand.

There is so much more to say, but I am going to stop right here. I want you to experience this book and get to know me as your coach, friend, and mentor, living her mission of helping thousands of entrepreneurs and knowledge-givers like you build an impactful and magnetic presence online through personal branding.

I want to help you get successful!

I'm rooting for you!

Your author, coach, and friend on the way,

– Diya Asrani

ACKNOWLEDGMENT

I would like to especially thank a few people without whom this book wouldn't have been possible.

My parents, Dr. Mukesh and Mrs. Renu Ramnane, for guiding me and pushing me beyond my comfort zone, and letting me experience things that have made me who I am today.

My sister, Roshni, for being the best younger sister and making me believe in myself.

My husband, Bharat, for guiding and supporting me at every step of the way. Without this man in my life, I don't know how I would be doing things that I thought I couldn't do.

My in-laws, Aarti and Suresh Asrani, for being so supportive and loving. I feel blessed to have them, too, like my parents. They have stood by me like pillars on this journey.

My clients, students, and community members for helping me live my mission by trusting me as their coach, trainer, or mentor.

A special thanks to my three mentors, Puja Puneet, Siddharth Rajsekar, and Rajiv Talreja, for not only guiding me on the way but also helping me become the person I am today. I would also like to thank them for sharing their wisdom in the 'Interview Diaries' section of each chapter in this book. Each word has added tremendous value to the entire book!

I would also like to especially thank the founder and CEO of India's leading training and coaching company, Success Gyan, Surendran

Acknowledgment

Jaysekar, for helping me gain experience from some of the finest coaches and trainers in the industry—some of whom are my mentors.

Last but not least, I want to thank you, my dear reader, for buying this book and living my story one chapter at a time. I hope you like it!

Take it all in, and let me show you the way.

Diya Asrani

1
THE "AHA!" MOMENT

The greatest eureka moment is discovering yourself

— Bangambiki Habyarimana

The year was 2004. It was 7:15 a.m. Roshni and I were getting ready for school, while Dad was hurrying us up, saying, "You're late, girls! Hurry up, or the bus will leave without you." I wore my uniform, strapped on my shoes, ate my favourite sandwich for breakfast, grabbed my lunch box that Mom patiently packed with a lot of love, and finally walked towards the gate.

Suddenly, I stopped and looked back. My dad asked me, "Now what happened, Diyu? What did you forget?"

"Papa, I'll just go upstairs and come. One minute." I rushed back to my room, skipping alternate steps, and stood right in front of my full-length mirror.

No, I wasn't heading to the washroom. How predictable are you!

And there, I asked myself, "Do I look good today?"

"Should I wear my skirt slightly above the knees?"

"Should I style my hair differently?"

"Oh, crap! I forgot to wear kajal!"

And there, I took another ten minutes, evaluating how I looked.

Now, this might look like I was the kind who would take ages to get ready for school every day. The truth is, I was not.

I was always so easy going with the way I dressed. And, anyway, that uniform was nothing fancy really. But I was definitely insecure and uncertain about how I looked.

Visualize this. White shirt, grey box-pleated skirt, dark-blue Nike shoes (yup, you read that right), and the school emblem right on the pocket on the chest. Still, wondering what the use of that pocket was!? And, of course, white socks to complete the look.

But there was always a feeling of void and insecurity when I would go to school and see how my friends would look so stylish in that not-so-fancy uniform. I would frequently ask myself, "Why don't I look good like them?"

This feeling of a void was something that lingered in my head for quite some time. At first, it felt like a natural feeling, that I am generally so carefree about my looks. But as the days passed, I started feeling more insecure. I had a lot more questions cropping up in my mind, and they only got more intense!

My mom started noticing my body language closely. And Mom, being the mom, asked me, "Diyu, what is troubling you? You are not yourself."

I just took a moment and then finally broke down into tears and blurt all these sentences. "They don't appreciate my presence."

"They don't like me."

"I don't have any friends."

"Is there something wrong with me?"

My mom immediately stopped me from saying those things and asked, "Are you getting your period?"

I yelled and said promptly, "No, Ma!"

"Okay. Okay! Calm down." She gauged the situation and said these golden words, "It's time you started taking care of yourself. You have bigger things to face in life; this is nothing. You have to start today… like NOW!"

So here's something about my mom. She has her own cute and creative ways of teaching Rosh & Me about life. She's more like a friend than a strict mom. Known for her chirpy personality, elegant style, and go-getter approach to life, she always managed to handle us like a boss lady.

Here's a secret. A lot of what I share with you in this book is because of my parents.

Let's talk about her style and presence. A lover of pastels, kitten heels, and breathable fabrics, and brewing with confidence that many of her friends would love to learn from her. The way one of the aunties would say, "Renu, how do you do it?" Still today, she does it with so much grace!

Still today, she believes that expressing yourself the right way, visually, is like unlocking a password for people to connect with you. Visual presence matters! And visual presence is not only about the clothes we wear but also about the confidence that we build, the body language we possess, manage our wellness, and all in all, how we want to be perceived by people.

To date, my dad, too, is of the opinion that your presence matters, and how you show yourself to the people around you is a sign of self-respect. Being a reputed doctor, he has always been of the opinion that things got to be simple yet professional.

Presence, the word we use so often, usually subconsciously, is so synonymous with how we go about living our day-to-day lives. You must've heard the following statements before and probably said them to yourself or someone around you.

"Your presence matters!"

"Make your presence felt."

"You need to build your presence."

"People should relate to your presence."

"Your presence is important in this meeting."

"Your presence changes so many things for the better!"

'Presence' is a word that has lived in our dictionary for years and continues to today. It's a conscious effort of doing and being in a certain way.

Pondering over this whole thought of 'Presence matters,' I started working on myself when I got out of high school. Was I conscious about my looks? Oh, yes! I kind of got obsessed with my presence to the extent that every day, I would wake up in the morning and tell myself, "Diya, your presence matters. Start working on it."

The first and most important thing to work on was my physical presence. I know times are different today, and people don't see 'being chubby' as a flaw. But when I was in school, I used to be very conscious of the fact that I was chubby. Not because people called me "Chubby," but because I used to find it difficult to cope with sports. My PT master would call me "Laddoo" because I would struggle to run fast or play any kind of sport.

So, as soon as I realized that this was something that won't take me anywhere, I switched gears…

And from there, it was an upward spiral to building my presence. Right from my style to building confidence to working on my posture to getting rid of my fear of public speaking and stage fright. Yes, it did take me years to work on myself, but it was worth it because, in the end, it really is about how you feel about yourself first.

About the so-called friends in school who looked better in that drab uniform? Ah! Well, that didn't bother me anymore.

Ever since then, I have literally carved and engraved this strong and significant belief of building my presence in my mind. Not only was I working on my physical presence, but I also, on the way, communicated and connected with people.

Once I started seeing the difference in myself, I realized that I was doing something right. I got more respect in school, my confidence skyrocketed in expressing myself, and I became more conscious about my surroundings. Overall, it was a win-win.

They say that the quality of what you do and how you live your life begin from your roots. And that's what I focussed on the most. It was like building a strong foundation for myself in order to grow gracefully in the years to come.

I would come back from school, and Mom would say, "See, your presence matters. So much change in *you*!" Without my mom and dad's support and the constant motivation to be better, I don't know where I would've been today.

As and when I started gaining confidence, I would frequently think about helping other girls look and feel better about themselves. But I used to wonder how I would be able to do this without being 'qualified' and experienced enough to do so.

During school days, impacting people and making a difference wasn't really a priority except in a classroom amongst your own peers. So I used to subtly talk about fashion, style, and dressing up during tea-break, and of course, the girls in my class would be curious about building their own style and presence but didn't know how to go about it.

We were never taught how to be confident when presenting ourselves in school. The priority was to do well in academics while understanding our culture and wearing the right uniform. Sad that our education system still and mostly believes in that.

After high school, I went to a well-known design school to study arts and then textile designing. Till today, I wonder why I chose to go to design school, and I remember being so excited and eager to take it up. But when I got into it, it was not a very smooth four and a half years of my life. Here's what it felt like. I had lost all of my confidence (again) because I was bullied quite a bit by my seniors. Then I ended up in a toxic relationship, wherein I got cheated on my first solo trip to Goa. It went on to me being pulled down by my so-called teachers, and to top it all, I had a strong fear of traveling alone by public bus because the school was really far, and an auto-ride would have cost me seven-hundred rupees a day! I was always in a hurry to come back home from school, as each day, I would feel my confidence getting weaker.

I didn't have the heart to tell my folks that I wanted to shift to a different school or just quit because it costed a bomb to get into that school in the first place.

Fast forward to 2011. It was finally the end of those four years, and I had grabbed the opportunity to switch careers from Textile Designing to Image Consulting. While doing some research, I found an exciting course on becoming an Image Consultant and Soft Skills Trainer. Of course, after those four years, all the work on my presence and confidence had gone down the drain. So, I did wonder if this new course would be of any use.

Since it was a one-year course, and that too only on weekends, I decided to take the plunge and see how it goes. While meeting and collaborating with people during this course, I started falling in love with the concept of presenting myself confidently. I learned and mastered every single topic taught in class and would apply the concepts to myself as and when I learned new ways of building my presence.

The "AHA!" Moment

After getting certified, I immediately got an opportunity to be one of the trainers at that institute. My confidence started coming back slowly and steadily. And while training and coaching so many people from various industries, my curiosity turned into research, which helped me understand what people really valued the most—One's Presence.

I started my journey as an Image Consultant and Trainer, helping people build their presence, increase their confidence, and just be their awesome selves when communicating with people. I still didn't really have a 'brand name' in mind, so people knew me by my name and soon would look at me as one of the go-to experts in Image consulting and training.

I was the brand, maybe?

But I still had a long way to go!

Fast forward to 2014. When I was working as a Stylist for Myntra, I was given this awesome opportunity of styling this famous designer's fashion show. The showstopper was the Indian actress, Sushmita Sen!

In conversation with the designer, I asked her one thing. "Rina, how would you like the look and feel of your show to be?" To this, she said, "Diya, you are the stylist. You should know more about the 'stage presence' of a person! Sushmita wants her presence to be natural. She would like to focus more on her own personal style."

There you go again. More about Presence!

The experience was a rollercoaster ride for me because this time, I had to work with someone who already knew her personal style but just wanted to highlight it on stage. And working with someone who already has a presence can be a challenge!

In 2015, I landed a job at this retail giant called Arvind Mills.

Familiar? Yes, of course, especially for us Indians. I was the Manager for Styling of their brand editorials and catalogues for their omnichannel 'nnnow.com.'

Here, I was involved quite deeply with the hoity-toity, fancy-schmancy brand managers who spoke so vividly about their brand! No jokes. Some of them actually talked like they 'owned' the brand!

Most of our long conversations hovered around similar lines like, "The point is, the brand presence needs to come out in the pictures!"

or

"You need to know more about our brand's language and presence to really understand how customers can relate to us." or

"The Presence of the Brand is all about a fun, carefree, free-spirited individual hanging out with his/her friends."

I have had many experiences like these: conversations with brand owners, clients, managers, designers, entrepreneurs, and many more. But I gathered that one's presence matters at every step in growing a brand, business, individual, or even a relationship.

So I started giving this a more serious thought and realized the scope in helping more people build their own presence. I started by coming up with a sketchy brand name for myself.

Attempt 1 – 2016

I called my brand 'Style Marché,' which means 'style market' for some vague reason. Why the name? Oh, well, I just liked it, and it sounded French! Didn't use it much, but yes, I tried really hard to make it work with what I did.

I started doing more photoshoots, getting involved with magazine editorials, creating my own shoots, and went on and on with trying to make Style Marché THE brand name for me.

Did I try too hard?

I also integrated fitness into this brand because I wanted to add another angle to the approach. More about this when I talk about the 'Unique Switch' in chapter four.

In 2017, I was given the pink slip because they were downsizing the company. That's when I actually woke up and realized that I was so much more than I thought. Losing my job was a really big change for me, especially when I knew I was good at it. With support from my parents, sister, and husband, I snapped out of it and soon started thinking about my future again.

The first thing I did was ditch the name 'Style Marché' and decide to build the brand 'Diya Asrani' because that is what people related to the most.

Here's something to keep in mind: people tend to remember your name for a longer time than your company name because they directly associate themselves with you first and then the company that you own.

People need to know who you are before they associate with the brand or programme you are offering.

A few months later, I decided to get coached by one of The Leading life coaches in India, Puja Puneet. During our second session, we were doing a brainstorming activity on how I should be designing a programme that would help entrepreneurs build their personal brand presence as trusted experts.

We started writing all the words that we could think of! Maybe close to a hundred words?

We looked at the list of words for a minute and…believe it or not, we both said, "Presence!" together!

Now how to make it sound classy and relatable?

"Diya, you help them design their 'presence' as an expert. So, let's keep it simple. Design Your Presence! That can be your brand name!" said Puja.

And there I go, "Aha!"

We had our mini moment of celebration, and that just opened more doors for me to telling people that I help Design Your Presence as a trusted and valuable expert in the industry!

That's how Design Your Presence was born! So quick. Like it was waiting to be discovered!

Today, the word 'presence' is synonymous with how I approach every single aspect of my brand, my lifestyle, and the way I project myself in front of people. My clients connect with me because of that word! And what's more amazing is that it's an absolute no-brainer when I have to talk about 'Design Your Presence.' Why? Because people get it!

Now that you know a little bit about how this all started, don't you think it is all about the journey and certain messages that come on the way to help you move in a certain direction?

Before we move to the next chapter, I would really like you to take a fresh notepad and pen (with lots of ink!) and answer these questions.

Do not just think about the answers, but actually write them down because they will just disappear after you turn the page.

Be honest, be real, and don't overthink.

Why did you buy this book? (What made you take this step? Why do you want to build your presence?)

What about your story that people should know? Write three turning points that you would like to share.

Describe your own version of your presence.

What do you want to be known for?

What are you passionate about and would like to help people with?

INTERVIEW DIARIES

When did you find your "Aha!" moment when it came to building your presence as a life coach?

Honestly, I was looking at helping my own self. In 2005/2006, I didn't know where I was heading. I got married at a very young age, and I was that typical young bride who did not get her education; I never went to college. I think I had lost myself. I became more of a mould of what my in-laws and parents wanted me to be. And then a day came when I realized I wanted to know who I was beyond all the labels put on me. And I think just by looking and searching for who I wanted to become, it became the journey of "Okay, this is how you do it!" And as I learned it step by step, I started noticing that people asked me how I did it.

I think the best student is the one who teaches while learning, and I felt I needed to teach others so that I could be a role model while doing the best for my own life. It was an impromptu start, and I didn't know the term 'Life Coach' even existed! I remember praying to god: "If I become happy, I will make other people happy."

I had lost that self-identity, self-esteem, and I feel most women go through this point when they feel enough is enough, that I'm tired of living for others, and it's time to live for myself. I think when you rediscover yourself, you automatically become an inspiration.

To put it all together, if you don't live your purpose, you can't become happy.

— Puja Puneet, Life Coach, Author, and CEO of *Life By Design*

2

THE BARBED BOUNDARY OF COMFORT

The comfort zone is the greatest enemy of courage and confidence

– Brian Tracy

The fact is anyone and everyone can be successful. Read that again. Your idea doesn't have to be extraordinary to be successful. An idea that's simple, economical, and easy to use can do the trick. What really is crucial is why and how did you get to the final outcome and what really made your concept a prominent choice for your audience.

The HOW doesn't mean only the process or strategy behind building your business; it is also a lot about taking the leap and getting things done anyway!

In other words, it is 'trespassing the barbed boundary of your comfort zone.'

We are usually very used to telling ourselves things like: "I would like to be comfortable in life," or "Comfort is more important than anything else!" or worse, "I want to be comfortable, have enough money, own a big house, drive a big car, but without having to do much."

But here's the fact. Being comfortable is overrated and often makes you feel accomplished for a very short while.

You got to step out of this safe zone and move into the zone of growth, creativity, and abundance to really achieve something great. Then you can talk about a big house, fancy cars, and enough money because then you earned it!

Remember I told you about my PT master calling me "Laddoo" (*a round Indian sweet that can actually transform you into a ladoo*) in school? I was always so petrified of playing sports. Whether it was playing basketball or participating in jungle gym races, I was always so scared because I thought I was really fat to do these things. Correction: I was, well, a *little* plump.

I was in sixth grade. We had our sports day coming up, and everyone had to take part in it. I still wonder today, what made them throw me into a 'jungle gym race.' Anyway!

A jungle gym race looks like this. I had to climb up the tall jungle gym and then jump down and then climb up again and repeat, pretending to be a monkey on fire. Sounds fun, right? Not!

There's a reason why jungle gyms are also known as monkey bars.

When it was my turn to practice, my PT master would call out, "Aye, Ladoo, it's your turn now. You need to do five rounds to complete the race." Have you seen a scared cat freeze, with her hair standing up like spikes? I was something like that, minus the hair. Shocked, lost, and scared to do that!

At the end of it, instead of feeling accomplished, I felt like he had forced me to do something I wasn't comfortable with. Thoughts like these came up in my mind:

"How can he call me fat and then make me do something so uncomfortable?"

"He is so cruel! He wanted people to make fun of me."

I went back home after school, feeling miserable. I spoke to my mom about it and expressed a deep sense of embarrassment, pain, and anger.

She asked me this one question that actually got me thinking.

"Diyu, you said you were embarrassed about doing something you thought you couldn't do. Why did you do it then?"

I paused and asked myself, "Why did I do it? I could've just skipped practice or, better, called in sick that day. But, *why* exactly did I do it?"

The 'Whys' usually give you the answers. Why are you doing what you are doing? Why did you do it even if you didn't enjoy it? Why did you do it in spite of people calling you names that you hated?

The story of this chubby girl is a clear example to understand that doing something uncomfortable allows you to understand your capabilities. And this is something I noticed very late in life.

Discounting the fact that I was a kid back then, and how I would ever figure out that this small experience would allow me to review it again while writing this book.

As I said before in this chapter, comfort zones are overrated. It is where your mind lives and lets you believe that this is what *needs* to be done. We often tell ourselves that we have to be safe on our journey to success. But there's a reason why it's called a 'success ladder.' Because ladders, though stable in their own ways, can also be a little challenging to climb just like the jungle gym.

We build our own notions of facing risks and uncomfortable situations. These notions are based on our strong belief in playing it safe. But what we don't see is that if we are playing our cards 'safe' in building a business that's bigger than us, we have already failed before we even started.

So here's some re-wiring of the mind for the chubby Diya in school.

"I broke the barbed wire of my comfort zone and actually did something I thought I couldn't do."

"I might have been called fat, plump, or 'Ladoo' by my PT master, but his main aim was not to bring down my confidence but to encourage me to get out of my comfort zone and just push myself to complete the race."

"I feel more confident and courageous after accomplishing this task, which once was a daunting thought that came my way."

"Being uncomfortable in my journey of being successful is the new normal."

Now think about your business. Your journey is going to be full of jungle gym races, diving into a swimming pool without learning how to swim, climbing tall mountains, and, well, more of doing things you aren't comfortable with and probably weren't ready for.

The fact is, you can never be ready. But that doesn't mean you'd stick around in your comfort zone. The reason why playing safe can be harmful to your growth is it doesn't show you your capabilities. You're made to believe that you have limitations, and you can't go beyond those.

Who told you that?

One answer: Your own voice.

The key is to challenge yourself and do things beyond the barbed wire. This means, break the rules, create new ones, do things differently, and create magic!

What does being passionate really mean? Doing things anyway out of excitement and energy. You cannot compromise on anything that relates to your passion, and that is what you need to tell yourself before you read the rest of this book.

Okay, so here's something for you to do. Make sure you attempt it before moving to the next chapter.

Here's the thing. If you decide to skip it, you have officially taken the safe route.

Pick something that you have *never* done before. Now don't treat this like a dare. Keep in mind that you are doing this to break the barbed wire. Here are some examples for you: 1. Cooked a meal; 2. Recorded a video and posted it on social media; 3. Washed the dishes; 4. Climbed a ladder and cleaned the fan. It can be anything, but make sure it is beyond your safe zone.

What not to do: something that risks your life. I don't need to elaborate on this one.

After the activity (Point 1), write down ten things that you can do to grow your business, on a fresh sheet of paper. Things that excite you, scare you, give you goosebumps. Or something that you never thought you could do. Write it. Don't stop yourself.

From the list, pick the top three things that you can do in the next ten days. These can be based on priority or scale (big to small).

Pledge that you will complete these in the next ten days.

INTERVIEW DIARIES

They say success is outside the comfort zone. What is your perspective on being uncomfortable when building one's presence online?

There are two things that I live by:

One, I believe that everything is figureoutable, as Marie Forleo says it. Start before you're ready! I have moved my business from offline to online, and there's so much I've had to learn. Following the fact that everything is figureoutable, I told myself that whatever comes my way is figureoutable! One of the biggest things I've let go of is perfecting everything. Like my friend Rajiv Talreja says, "Success is Shabby," I believe it's been my biggest learning in the year 2020.

The other thing is, earlier, my definition of confidence was to keep taking small risks and accomplishing them. Today, it's about showing up anyway. And if things go wrong, I'll be able to handle it.

New identity needs new evidence, and we need to project that new evidence.

– Puja Puneet, Life Coach, Author, and CEO of *Life By Design*

3

MOULDING YOUR JOURNEY

The only impossible journey is the one you never begin

— Tony Robbins

I once overheard my principal at school say, "Success is only at the end of the road. It is something that you achieve only after years of studying, excelling in exams, and then getting a lucrative job."

This makes me wonder. If success is about the result, what about all the work that happens on the way? Aren't we heading somewhere? Are we doing something that makes us progress in life?

Progress. That's the word, my friend.

When you progress in anything that you want to do, you are also creating a journey that helps you move towards your goal. That journey is the success in itself!

Think about the people who inspire you. How did they get where they are? Why are you inspired in the first place? And have they stopped doing what they are doing because they are successful? Absolutely not. They still work. They still inspire. They still constantly work on themselves. They are constantly doing things to get to the next step.

They don't believe in creating a happy ending, like it is in a movie. They live their lives like a movie, and when it is actually the end of the road, they have completed their mission and built that legacy that allows people to remember them to date. Take Steve Jobs. Take Michael Jackson. Take Stephen Hawking. Don't we still talk about them today?

Do you know the secret? You can do this too. You can build a legacy. No jokes. Each one of us has something special. A gift that we can share with the world. Remember my "Aha!" moment. Don't doubt the fact that you have it too. I wouldn't be surprised if you have already found your "Aha!" moment.

Moulding your journey is like treating your life like clay. It is really up to you to create, design, and nurture it. When you take the leap and break the barbed wire of your comfort zone, you decide to be successful and not settle for anything less. Your journey is the story that allows you to tell people why you're doing what you're doing, fearlessly.

When I found out that designing people's personal brand presence is what makes me feel complete, I decided to open multiple routes to my destination, test it out with people, and just get things up and running.

It was a really slow start, though.

Slower than a slug. But it was worth it.

I started from training people at companies and helping employees position themselves better to working with college students and getting them job-ready to finally, helping entrepreneurs, coaches, and trainers build their brand presence by inviting them to my exclusive masterclasses.

When you decide to be a creator of something that drives you, you are automatically respecting the fact that you are more than what it takes. In my initial days of coaching and training, I never used to really believe in the fact that I needed to build a business that revolved around my passion. My initial years were all about: "Let's take it as it comes," or "Let's see how it goes" or worse, "Let me first recover the money I have spent on the course and then aim for success." Dream tarnishing? Indeed.

I always thought that business was for those people who were certified to do it and could afford to invest in building a business on a large scale. I called them the 'Elite Business People.' But I didn't realize that, by thinking this way, I was literally crushing my dreams and limiting myself to what I believed in.

These thoughts led me to take the wrong decisions, which turned out to be nice stories to tell later on. One is my two-year stint at a very well-known retail company. Yes, I decided to help someone else on their mission to make a difference in the world, which kept my mission on the back burner, unknowingly and unintentionally.

Why did I decide to take up that job? It required me to style and manage some of the biggest brands in the world. A few of them were Sephora, Arrow, GANT, GAP, Tommy Hilfiger, Elle, U.S. Polo, Nautica. This was the hook. It was almost like living my dream bigger and better than I had thought.

But I forgot my own mission, goals, and brand building in the process. Just to make myself feel like I was doing some work, I would work on my so-called brand every weekend. And if you define "work on the brand," for me, in those days, it was somewhere close to a quick Google search on a topic, working on aimless presentations, and then dreaming about the future, which seemed far-fetched to me.

Fast forward to the year 2017. I was coming back after a long and blissful vacation in Europe and London with Bharat, my better half. We were reminiscing and going through some of our favourite moments from the holiday when a spark of curiosity made me quickly check my work-mail before take-off. I did feel a tingling sensation of nervousness as if there was a little war going on in my stomach, not because I knew what was to come, but because I was fearful about what I've missed out on while I wasn't around. I didn't even anticipate what I was going to hear from my colleagues or boss.

When I tried logging in to my account, it said: "Access denied." I tried again, and I got a message saying that the account did not exist anymore. I took a deep breath and gave it another try and then another. My fingers started trembling, and I felt a sort of heaviness in the head. It was as if a pile of stones was dropped on it. I was sweating!

I then texted Tanuja, my colleague and friend, asking her if she could help me out. She gave me the shocking update of the company getting downsized.

And that's it. I saw something coming!

My journey back home was a four-hour project of deep thinking "What next?" thoughts, and a good amount of discussion with Bharat. I was still very positive about not being one of those people who had to leave the job. Because, honestly, I never compromised on the quality of work, nor did I disrespect the work culture of the company. In fact, I was an asset to them in many ways.

Anyway, the next morning, I woke up with the piercing feeling of uncertainty and clouded thoughts. I dressed my very best, wore the new shoes that I had bought in London, and headed to work, behaving as if everything was normal and nothing had happened. But in my mind, I was facing something that was nothing less than a turmoil. It was almost as if a mix of emotions were gushing in and out of my mind, battling with the way I was expressing myself visually. I definitely knew that something was amiss, and I had to just face it.

Remember I always believe in 'presence'? In this case, my visual presence had to support the situation like a pillar of support. Happy from the outside, shattered from the inside.

I got to the office, and in two hours, I was asked to leave the job. But because my boss and colleagues loved me, and they really had no choice but to let me go, they gave me a send-off instead. A very nice way of getting fired! Apparently, doesn't happen very often.

The minute I got back home, I felt a strange mix of feelings of satisfaction, uncertainty, happiness, and sadness. I was happy because I got the experience; I was sad because now I was in a situation, wherein I had no income flow. Suddenly, the word 'stability' disowned me, and I went into my shell for a few days.

What hit me the hardest? I had no plan B. The brand that I was working on every Saturday wasn't solid enough to help me financially. Now, here's the thing. I am not one of those people with no family support, no home to stay in, or anything like that. I had all the love and support that I needed during that time and still do to date.

But my priority was to stand on my own feet. From the time I left school, I have always had the dream to create something big that I'd be known for. I obviously didn't have so much clarity or a set goal, but I knew I had to make it big and do really well in whatever I chose. As long as I understood the fulfilment of making money through what I love, it was evident that my aim was to make sure I didn't rely on anyone for financial support.

My dad always says these words to me, still today, "Always remember, you chose to do this. You chose to work and build something big. Hard work pays, always. Don't worry if they asked you to leave. It doesn't end here. There are bigger opportunities in-store and even bigger challenges to face on the way. This is a constant journey that you have to mould!"

My dad is an extremely hardworking man and a very well-known Dermatologist in Bangalore. His philosophy has always been that we need to earn in order to understand the value of money. So, keeping that in mind, I restarted working on my own brand.

This time, not by working on someone else's mission. I reworked on my own mission, rebranded myself, and started building an actual business with zero experience in business management. Was I good? No way.

Was I doing something that made me happy and content?

Absolutely!

My mission to help people design their personal brand presence was getting amplified every single day. I was not making much money, but I was creating something that I could call mine. And this helped me confidently believe that I was earning enough every month. Of course, this was not an easy journey, as it took me months to rewire my mind and think beyond the whole idea of making money.

There was a point when I decided to become a Zumba Instructor so I could make money by conducting group classes.

I kept telling people around me that I had decided to convert my passion for Fitness and Dancing into a career. But inside, I was lying to myself.

I love fitness, I love dancing, and both are my crazy passions since I was a kid. But since I wanted to make money, I tried to make this a part of my mission. I tried to make sense of it, but I guess I tried too hard.

Here's something to think about. Don't do anything in a hurry, or if the reason is shallow and has no definite meaning to it. Because then, you only go down the funnel of failure. And that was what was happening to me.

In the next chapter, we will be talking more about this.

While I started conducting group classes, I slowly started moving away (again) from my main mission of helping people build their personal brand presence. The "Aha!" moment would go missing in my Zumba music. Not a good sign really.

I got involved in this form of fitness to the extent that I bought the most expensive Zumba merchandise, collaborated with other instructors, and got myself certified in multiple forms of Zumba training.

In a couple of months or so, I started losing interest in Zumba. I figured that my calling had more to do with personal branding, presence building, uplifting people, and helping them become better versions of themselves. Though I had my Zumba membership going for a while, I was only doing it for the 'side hustle' sake.

One day, I sat down and wrote a letter to myself. I call it the 'future me' letter.

It was a letter from Future Me to Current Me, wherein Future Diya was telling Current Me to mould my journey better and focus on things that meant to me. It looked something like this.

Dear Diya,

Life is really precious, and you have already come so far. Don't make choices that aren't allowing you to grow in your own mission. I would like to share the journey that got me to where I am, and I know you want to reach here soon. The view from the top is so amazing; I know you will enjoy every bit of it.

I realized that I need to focus on the bigger picture and take action accordingly. I have helped thousands of entrepreneurs, trainers, and coaches build their presence by building the quality of my own brand presence through the way I share my stories. To positively influence people around you, you first need to influence yourself to focus on your own mission.

You love working with people's presence, so why not dive deep, research, and see what they really need.

What also got me here is my eagerness to learn every day. I got myself coached by some really good experts in the industry. Maybe you should consider that too.

Diya, I know you're good at what you do, and your intentions are clear. Why not make the most of it?

Yours lovingly,

Future Diya

I immediately got cracking with building my brand 'Diya Asrani' as a Personal Branding Coach & Image Expert, leveraging the various experiences in training and coaching different people from various industries in the past few years.

I worked with many corporate and retail brands to understand their brand language that actually got me thinking that it is really about the people who connect with you. Their vision, their mission, and most importantly, their story. This was way bigger than Zumba classes, and spending on Zumba-wear wasn't my personal style!

I started penning down reasons as to why I wanted to build my brand.

Why do I want to be a positive influencer?

How do I position myself as a prominent expert and leader?

One answer: Take the leap of faith and do things that you thought you couldn't do.

I am sharing this with you because you need to know that moulding your journey lies only in your hands.

Every single experience you have and every single connection you create triggers a sense of resonation that you might not figure out initially in your career, but, on the way to your goal, you will definitely find it if you are really searching for a deeper meaning behind what you are doing.

Look at Walt Disney, for example. He was always so keen to learn how to draw and create art with mediums like crayons and watercolours. And his constant curiosity about cartooning and illustrating got him to discover animation. He started his studio called Laugh-O-Gram Studio, which specialized in fairy-tale animation. He had a financial backer for a short while, but once the backer went broke, he couldn't pay his animators, which led his company into bankruptcy. But he didn't stop. He continued his journey by opening The Walt Disney Studio with his brother and expanding his horizons in the amusement park industry and whatnot! Think about his journey. Where did he start? Did he quit? Did he stop when his company went into bankruptcy? He actually took this as an opportunity to make bigger things happen in his life. The famous character of Mickey Mouse is the popular USP (unique selling proposition) that people remember him for. His movies such as Cinderella, Mary Poppins, The Lion King, and more are watched with so much love and interest not only by children but also by adults like you and me. The key here is, he moulded his own journey, and he had a passion that led him to create a mission bigger than himself.

If you are trying to build something meaningful, always remember that it only depends on how you mould your journey and take the next step. If you are giving up because it is challenging, feel free to question your level of passion. If you feel like taking the easier route, let me be honest with you, you are already on your way down the hill.

I made those mistakes in my life. I tried everything that made me move away from my main mission, but I snapped back, understanding that the drive to help people design their presence was a constant magnetic force that I couldn't let go of and that it was here to stay. In the process, I learned that it would take more than just making money. And so it took guts, power, and hard work to get to where I am today. I still call myself a "work in progress" because I believe I can do much more.

While reading this book further, you are going to feel the same! You will have all kinds of emotions cross your mind, thoughts that will make you wonder, ideas that will make you dream because that is just a simple understanding that you are moulding your journey, and it is going to make you do things beyond your imagination.

Even if you are reading this book ten years later, you are still on your way to building a legacy, and the journey starts fresh every single day!

My mission is to help you understand that you have more than you think you do to offer the world. Something that positions you as an expert who can be trusted. If you have reached this page of the book, I would like to personally thank you from the bottom of my heart for pushing yourself to convert your passion into a gift that you can share with people around you.

You, my friend, are living my mission to build passionate business creators and trusted experts!

Before moving to the next chapter, I want you to pause and do this quick exercise to help you be more aware of your score on the 'Scale of Passion.'

One being the lowest and ten being the highest, rate the following statements.

This Passion can define who I really am and what I love doing.

This Passion can help people around me.

The journey I have been through was all related to my Passion.

I can answer any question regarding this Passion.

I can create something that typically works around this Passion.

This Passion can bring out my personality.

The legacy I will be creating will revolve around this Passion.

I can convert this Passion into a Business.

I have sweet dreams about this Passion.

I have zero doubts about this Passion.

Result:

1–3 = You need to rethink the Passion. Do a self-talk session and reason out why and what else are you passionate about? If it makes it easier for you, write to me at info@diyaasrani.com with your doubt or question.

4–7 = You are a bit uncertain and need to build your confidence to take the leap. Notice where you have scored yourself less, and see how you can work on increasing it to the next level.

8–10 = You know you are cut-out for this, and you can confidently mould your journey around the certainty of success and appreciation of what you create!

INTERVIEW DIARIES

How was your experience at the start of building your business online?

The starting of my entrepreneurial journey was when I lost my job in 2011. I had to decide whether to get back to doing a job or start a business. I clocked in eight years in the digital world. I am not a graduate, so I worked my way up through my passion to learn. And I was surrounded by good people. I had good support from my bosses, who encouraged me to grow and learn on the way. Then I got the pink slip, and I had to decide whether to apply for a job or get into entrepreneurship. I decided to dive into the entrepreneurship world, and when I started my journey, it was exciting. But I was really nervous as I did not know what to expect. I've seen my dad and grandpa run their businesses, but I could not really understand what was going on inside.

I had to rediscover myself, and that included doing a lot of courses and learning new skills in the initial phase. Luckily, I had a business partner and a few mentors along the way. A lot of education happened in the Business Network International (BNI) circle, which I was a part of for five years. Then I had to get good at understanding the sales process, and from there, I moved on to learning how to make video proposals. I cracked a few deals doing these proposals. Then there was no looking back. I got better at it by the day and started enjoying this journey more and more.

The journey was great, but I faced a few challenges in the process.

There was no freedom in the business. I wanted to be my own boss, but I ended up having thirty-five bosses! My clients became my bosses. It really affected my health in 2015/2016. I suffered a panic attack; I couldn't sleep for two weeks. It was a tough situation. I was working in Bangalore. There was a lot of juggling with the family and all this going on.

The churn of clients and making ends meet. I would end up paying everyone. But as an entrepreneur, I wasn't satisfied with how much I paid myself. This was the case for many years. But there was hope, and finally, in 2018, I changed things for myself and transitioned from a service-based to a product-based model, wherein I raked in lots of profits, with a lean and mean team without any overheads.

– Siddharth Rajsekar, India's leading Digital Coach & Lifestyle Entrepreneur

4

THE BURNING DESIRE

You can't find your passion, thinking about it in your head

— Marie Forleo

We are conditioned to believe that we should know it all and be good at everything we do from the time we are born. Each task we do must emit the overwhelming 'fragrance' of perfection. So much so that they would even say, "You should be perfect in every single thing you attempt." Remember our school teachers? Especially when it comes to Indian education, they believe that every student must be perfect by scoring high in even the weakest subject. And if you are an all-rounder, you are cut-out for every single challenge in life. Really? I wish children today would question their teachers about this. It would be fun.

When I was in school, I wasn't a great student at all. And when it came to math, let's not even talk about it. I feel bad that my dad had to literally drill the math sense into my clueless brain. I finally had to join tuition classes that would actually simplify the already simple concepts to the extent that I had to literally attempt repeatedly until I got it right. My teacher was this jovial and respectable Bengali man with a healthy moustache and slick combed hair soaked in mustard oil. I remembered that smell every time I went to class. Not a great smell, to be honest!

Mr. Chatterjee made math so much fun for me, but once I got out of class, I would remind myself that the subject was and never would be my forte.

During one of our conversations, I asked him, "Sir, is it normal to dislike math as a subject? I mean, I am not passionate about it!"

He looked at me and gave one of those smiles and said this one thing in his thick Bengali accent, which rings in my head still today. "Diya, you need to have the '*bhaarning desirreee*' (burning desire) to do well in anything. If you don't have the desire, you can forget about being successful."

At first, I was a little lost, trying to resist myself from the sense of those words, but then it struck me. Isn't it true that only when you have the desire to do something great will you do a good job of it? Still today, I believe in that. Mr. Chatterjee did plant this thought in my mind in a way to tell me that if you have the passion to do well, or do something good, you will achieve it.

I scored 82% in math in my tenth-grade ICSE exams, which is pretty damn good considering I was failing miserably in all my previous exams.

Now, this doesn't mean I *am* passionate about math. Of course not! If you ask me to solve a math formula or calculate numbers in my mind spontaneously, I would probably judge you for being such a bully. Don't play your math tricks on me!

On the other hand, I was passionate about art. I still love it.

My art teacher in school, Mr. Mallesh, would teach something new every single day, and I would enjoy practicing it until I was satisfied with the outcome. I learned various techniques in art. From sketching to painting with acrylic paint and watercolours to colouring with dry pastels, it was quite clear that I had the patience to master each technique in art instead of solving word problems in math. I scored 98% in my tenth-grade ICSE exam.

Now, I wanted to share this example to help you understand that the desire to achieve something great has to be stronger than your existence. Imagine if we apply the same thing to what we love doing in life.

Imagine if you were to start a business or brand, you would be outstanding at it if you were passionate about it!

I was not passionate about math as a subject, but my desire to do well led me to do whatever it took to get that 82%.

I was, and still am, passionate about art as a subject, and the burning desire to be outstanding at it got me to excel in it! So the key is to excel in what you do, and it becomes a lot easier when you love what you do.

Now imagine if I was passionate about math as a subject and loved every single thing about it. I probably would've scored a 100% in the same without even getting tutored by Mr. Chatterjee. But having him teach me math was one of the best things that happened to me in my school days because he also shared a lot of his wisdom, which I apply today in my life.

Now, coming to our passions. I feel that many of us get stuck in the midst of a bouquet of passions we have. It sounds like this: "I love dancing. I enjoy traveling around the world. I love to sing. I love painting. I enjoy being fit. Oh, I also enjoy growing my own vegetables and dishing out fancy meals. I would love to own a pet salon." Now, this sounds awesome, and it is great to love and do so many things. But can you give your 100% to each one of them? Your answer might be a big YES! But once you actually get down to doing all these things with full force, you find that you are tiring yourself.

I call this 'Multi-Passion Paralysis (MPP),' a condition that each one of us have in different degrees. There is absolutely nothing wrong with having a number of passions. But what is wrong is trying to give your cent percent to every passion at the same time in the hope of growing each passion into a profession.

We tend to get stuck in this dilemma of being good at every single thing we love doing, and if we don't do it, we beat ourselves to it. This ends in paralyzing us and not letting us move ahead in the required direction.

Has this happened to me? Oh, yes! Many times. There was a time when I wanted to focus on all the passions and build one big business around it, forcing each of them to work with the other. For example, if I'm focusing on building personal brands, I thought of integrating Zumba classes to help keep people fit. And if they also wanted to elevate their home interiors, I could create custom-made paintings for them. Sounds really good when you think about the concept. I actually started working on my business, keeping this concept in mind, but little did I know that it would actually make me struggle more in growing my presence in a particular specialization.

Now, here's the onset of MPP. I started ideating the brand operations, story, strategy, and all the necessary elements to build the foundation. When it came down to explaining the "WHY" of my brand and bringing in the 'unique' aspect of my services, I couldn't articulate my concept in simple words.

It looked something like this.

In 2017, after getting fired and then trying to start over again, I started visiting all kinds of networking events. I had attended a BNI event, and as to how the protocol works, you have to introduce yourself and tell them what you do.

A senior member introduced me. "Let's welcome Diya to our chapter today. Diya, please introduce yourself."

MPP Me began, "Hey, everyone! I am Diya Asrani. I am a Personal Branding Coach, Artist, Zumba Instructor, Pound Fitness Instructor, and a corporate trainer. I integrate all these services to help people build their presence in all aspects."

Of course, people were impressed. Some of them personally congratulated me on being multi-passionate. But there were a few who questioned my approach towards building my business. Something as simple as "You are so passionate, Diya! But I would like to understand, what do you specialize in? Who would come to you, and what would they experience as a service?"

What was my answer?

"Oh! People from all walks of life can come to me for anything that relates to their presence! If they want to build a brand or get a custom-made artwork or lose weight and look good, anything! I have solutions for everything."

I thought I aced it with that answer. But little did I know that I had actually created an overwhelming picture in that lady's mind. She nodded as if she was impressed, but the conversation stopped short right there. "That's great! Thanks, Diya. Lovely talking to you. I wish you all the best in your multi-passionate venture!"

Proud as I could be, that evening felt great. Like an achievement of telling a small part of the world how good the business concept was and how creative it sounded to target absolutely ANYONE. The funny part is that I also had a dream of getting hired by a big multinational company, and I did. They offered me a 'Triple-Powered' project of getting their employees to build a brand, get fit, and develop an eye for designing and art!

Sounds like power puff girls in one body? Why not!

Now here's the thing. This might sound like a legitimate idea of multiple streams of income under one business. But in the end, if you're looking to have ways and means to stabilize your income, it has to be something that grows your business instead of compromise on its true ability to serve people in the most convincing way. In other words, you don't mess with the "WHY" of your brand presence by trying to build something that doesn't relate with many people, except for you, because you feel this might make you earn that extra money.

The key? Keep It Simple!

How do you do the 'KIS' test? Explain your mission to a ten-year-old child. If he or she understands it, you have won. If not, make it more simple!

Post that networking event, an array of thoughts flashed in my mind. I got asked so many times by so many people the golden question when anyone starts a business.

"Diya, WHY are you doing this?"

The thoughts, questions, and conversations got me to dive deeper into coming up with a valid answer to this question.

Was there something wrong with what I had said at the event?

Not really.

But here's the mistake that I made.

I didn't really 'specialize' in something while introducing myself. To put this into perspective for you, I compromised on the intensity of my brand presence!

I brainstormed my way into understanding why I was really doing that, and the words 'Burning Desire' popped up on my A3-size mind-map. Along with those words, helping people, better versions, confidence building, self-expression, creativity, and more came up, and that's when I felt that maybe I shouldn't be all over the place!

I asked myself these questions, and you can too!

What is that ONE thing I love doing that gives me that 'burning desire' of being outstanding at it?

What defines me as an expert, and how can I help people through this one thing I love?

What makes me different from the others? Is it my approach, my skill set, the way I talk?

What makes me stand out, can't be copied, and definitely can't be faked?

It is something that helps people choose *me* over the others in the industry. Now, this was not about competition. It had a lot to do with how I positioned myself as an expert in my industry.

Everyone has a skill, quality, or approach that makes them stand out in the industry, but they don't realize it at times. Here's why.

People constantly telling them that they aren't good enough or fit for the role.

They haven't been told that diving deeper into ONE passion is what really grows into a business.

They believe that being in the comfort zone and not taking risks is the key to successful businesses.

They copy others.

They feel the easier way out is the best way.

They feel being simple sucks.

They feel they are not cut-out for success.

Please do me a favour. Take a pencil and cancel those points right now! These few growth barriers are what is stopping you from building a presence that people want to know more about.

Here's something to think about:

Passion = Power + Unique Presence

Unique Presence = Niche + Creation + Positioning

If you understand this formula and how it works, designing your own presence won't be a challenge anymore!

The stronger the passion, the more unique you are in the eyes of your audience. What really makes you feel strongly about what you do?

It is the way you approach it and then master it. It starts with multi-level research, reading books, creating strategies, designing your positioning, designing programmes to share knowledge creatively, marketing and branding yourself hygienically, and most importantly, being your authentic self.

Being uncomfortable is the new normal while building something that will define you and support you when you are not around.

Think of Steve Jobs. People talk about him and his work to date. Being the pioneer of the personal computer era to co-founding Apple, he had his share of struggles on the way. But did those struggles stop him? Clearly not. Right until his last days in 2011, he was active in streamlining and digging deeper into how Apple could stand out in technology and be as versatile as it is today. To date, he is looked at as a trusted expert in his industry, even when he isn't physically around.

Wouldn't you want people to remember you for the impact you make through your creations?

Imagine that you are to attend a networking event and would need to introduce yourself in just one sentence. Write it down in the format below:

Hey, I'm (your name)

I'm a (designation), and I help (target audience) in/with/build/grow (focus area) through (passion), which allows them to achieve (goal).

OR

You can write it in your own words, but make sure you mention the following:

- Your name
- Your designation
- Target audience
- Focus area (For example, business growth)
- Passion
- End goal

INTERVIEW DIARIES

There are many non-techie entrepreneurs aspiring to grow their business online. Please share five actionable tips for them to get started without being overwhelmed.

I think the first step is to drop the tags like: "I'm not tech-savvy, I'm a non-techie, etc." Whenever you say "I am…," it distances you from learning anything new.

The second step is to be very clear on what your objective is. In other words, what is the deeper mission of your business? What kind of impact do you want to make?

For example, when you set a destination on Google Maps, it gives you the route. If there's a roadblock, it is going to find a detour and give you another route to the destination. Once you know where you want to go, you'll automatically know where you don't want to go. The problem with entrepreneurs is that they are not clear about their destination. So, everything becomes shiny in the digital world, and they end up consuming so much information that they get overwhelmed.

The third step is to follow one mentor and follow his/her system without getting distracted by other ways to do it. Follow that system, take it to the finish line, and then look for other possibilities.

The fourth step is to be in the game. You cannot score runs by sitting in the pavilion. Now, how fast you score runs is irrelevant, as long as you don't get out. So, in the digital world, it's about learning the tools, being hands-on, learning marketing, and basically being in the game before you can start to outsource them later on.

This leads me to the fifth step—scaling up. The only way you can do this is when you have hands-on knowledge about what's possible. Scalability can be in multiple ways: you can automate your systems, delegate them to internal teams, or even outsource them to external teams.

Once you do this, you get enough time to work on what you are good at and on the skills that you need to work on further.

– Siddharth Rajsekar, India's leading Digital Coach & Lifestyle Entrepreneur

5

THE SUCCESS SECRET: SPECIFICITY

No niche is too small if it's Yours!

– Seth Godin

There are over a thousand secrets to success that can make you think more and more about how you can and should approach your business concept and brand presence. But there is one thing that solves the problem of "how to stand out in my industry." And that's this: getting specific with what you do.

Being a trainer and coach for many years, I was always told that I can be an 'expert' in every topic and be ready to solve any problem that people throw at me. I felt like a so-called 'guru' who had to make things work for everyone through my magic words! Many of us have this misconceived notion of being an expert. We tend to call ourselves experts in many things because it sounds great. But the truth is, we can't please everyone. That's why it is important to be an expert in a specific topic.

The power of focusing on ONE topic that we're ready to laser-like focus on is a straight road to mastering it. Each topic, concept, or skill has enough and more scope to be explored and mastered by each one of us.

The fact is that there is lots of work to do for everybody.

Remember, if you really want to make an impact, you have to prioritize what your audience really wants from you. They want to see what it is that you can bring to the table that would benefit them in the long run.

The challenge is not in planning the dive but actually finding the right treasures when you reach the deepest point in the ocean. In simple words, if you have the best solution for just one big problem that needs to be solved, you have won.

Deep? Oh, yes, that's how becoming an expert in your 'niche' should really be. Playing in the shallow waters isn't really going to help you move ahead in what you are passionate about.

Okay, so what really is a niche?

A profitable and focused approach towards products and services that cater to a relevant audience.

Let's make this simple for you. There are absolutely ZERO shortcuts in finding your niche. It is literally one of the first steps in defining your personal brand presence. It is what you're known for in the industry and, more importantly, where the money really is! Did you know that the only person who can actually convert a niche into a money churning machine is you? So, please be sure that any niche you explore, if done well, can bring you success in your business.

Figuring out what you really stand for and how you can play a part in your audience's life will open doors to opportunities that will only enable you to grow in the industry. Many entrepreneurs find it extremely complicated to find a niche that they want to work on. Maybe so! But if it were so simple, the whole idea of 'creating a business' or 'specializing in a topic' would never have been so exciting.

There are so many times that entrepreneurs think that niching it down would actually decrease the number of opportunities coming their way. When the truth is, the deeper you go to find your niche, the more likely you are to increase your impact in the industry. Gone are the days of proudly saying that you can help with any topic and solve any problem for anybody you meet.

Being specific and specializing in something is the need of the hour and, more importantly, our duty to do so. Why I say it is a duty? It is because it is the golden ticket to giving ourselves the opportunity to make a positive difference in people's lives.

Here's a point to consider.

Impacting five people in your target audience of a hundred is more meaningful and rewarding than sharing information with a thousand people who don't really connect with you.

The sad truth is that we pay more attention to the number of people who follow and listen to us and very less to that 1% who are really finding value in what we do.

And when we focus on the wrong things, it reflects in the growth of the business. I'm sure you would not want that happening, especially when you've built and nurtured your passion from the ground up.

Being in the industry for so many years, I was doing my bit of spreading knowledge as an Image Consultant, a trainer, and a speaker, utilizing all the necessary soft-skills training material, a huge content library of literally all the topics that existed as necessary skills for anyone looking to improve themselves.

I have travelled around India to train employees of some of the biggest companies like the Indian School of Business, CapGemini, and Zee Group. The experience was great overall, but I was never 100% satisfied with what I was doing. I can say that the work was appreciated. I can also say that I did mess up in many places, which is a part of the journey, but it taught me a lot. But it wasn't satisfying to me at all. The only thing I saw coming in was the money, which was, again, not something to be proud of, but that was the only thing that kept me going.

After my stint at Arvind brands in 2017, while going through the entire phase of starting all over again, I figured out that personal branding was my calling because it was something that accumulated topics from image management, soft skills, and overall business growth. Since I was on this not-so-smooth journey of building my personal brand all those years, I felt the connection with the idea of branding myself to build a reputation in my industry. I also fell in love with the fact that personal branding is more a journey of growing and nurturing a business rather than just being a brand that exists. Right from self-exploration to reading, then to finally getting my answers from my mentor and coach, I created my own interpretation of finding one's niche—The 'DIVE' Strategy into the 'Niche Trench.'

Putting it into perspective, this strategy makes it simple to initiate the thought process in one direction that leads to the core of what you are really known for.

The 'DIVE' Quotient, inspired by the love of the sea and the dream to go deep-sea diving (well, someday!), is what I call the most realistic way of beginning your niche discovery.

Okay, so how does this work? It is very simple. A strategy that's rated zero is the fluff and complicated approach, and a BIG ten on ten is for the no-fuss and realistic approach.

In the end, it is about strategies that are doable, right?

When you want to understand what you specialize in, it is always good to know how much you are willing to take it forward. So here goes.

D – Discover – Which industry would you want to focus on? Is it something that you resonate with? This is important because once you know what you really want to discover, the rest of the steps become simpler.

I – Intention – What is your goal that makes you proudly share your message with people? What do you want them to gain from you?

V – Vehicle – In that industry that you had discovered, what would you want to focus on? What is that topic that you can specialize in?

E – Emphasis – How deep can you go into this topic? Are you willing to explore and discover findings on this topic?

Once you have figured out your 'DIVE' strategy, you can start testing the waters before the final dive into the Niche Trench.

By testing waters, I mean actually applying your 'DIVE' strategy and practicing it, testing it out, and researching it to see how you can approach it better.

I created this method, keeping the irony of diving deep into absolutely anything if you really want to find the right answers. In other words, be a focussed explorer who really has done the work and now has the solution.

People dislike ambiguous messages that have no meaning.

They really want to understand what you do, in simple words. Look at this example.

Version 1 – I help people increase their income by designing online courses that are valuable and easy to follow. Version 2 – I help people create online courses.

Notice the details in version 1? Which one would you choose?

Let's take my example here.

D – Discover – In all my years of experience, I discovered that what really excites me is the process of growing and nurturing a business. I don't have any certificate, a degree in business management, but through coaching, mentoring, and continuous learning from various sources, I figured out that it's something that I enjoy doing. Creating a business that grows and then helping others do it was what I wanted to do. It took me some time to understand that I actually love the idea of business growth, but often I would take the back seat and not do much about it. But when this became my calling, I started moving in this direction that got me to find my niche in this vast industry.

I – Intention – While I dreamt about making it big and standing on my own feet, earning loads of money, and building a presence that people find valuable, my intention has always been to help people like me—entrepreneurs and knowledge-givers—build their reputation and fearless presence as phenomenally prominent leaders in their industry. That has been the goal, the final destination of everything I do. Why? Because that's what I focussed on when I was growing my business, and I continue to do it as I write this.

V – Vehicle – Now, when it comes to the vehicle, here's something that you need to understand. To get to your destination, it's really not about just discovering what you like. It is also about creating a path that leads to the destination. Something that you use as a tool to get things working. Something that specifies what you're an expert in.

So things don't stop at just discovering something and then figuring out the intention. There has to be something that you focus on, something specific within your discovery, but what you can focus on and get good at. That 'something' is your vehicle. That something is your focussed topic of expertise under your large discovery. So, for me, in business growth, with an intention to build one's reputation, my focussed topic is Branding. It's my vehicle that I use to help people grow their business, which then leads them to build their fearless presence as reputed experts in their industry.

E – Emphasis – Okay, now that I know my vehicle in what I've discovered and have a solid intention, I need to further emphasize on what I am good at doing in Branding. Could it be graphic designing, building websites, content strategy, typography, digital branding, employee branding, corporate branding, or personal branding? Oh, wait! It is Personal Branding! There you go. I emphasize on personal branding, and this is what I help people develop so that they can present themselves online as phenomenally prominent leaders.

So, do you see how my message is slowly and steadily developing? The more specific we get, the more relatable our message becomes.

In my early days of doing business, I was always so vague about my message. I would only focus on generalizing the topic without a strong intention or vehicle to take things forward. People don't care about your message. Their first question is, "What makes *you* different from *them*?" or "Why should I choose you for this service? What can you do differently for me?" Do you see the words? What can you do differently? How can you dive deep into what you do and really pull out the real meaning and purpose behind the service or product you're offering?

People don't need the fluff. There's already enough around you. You can do things differently if you really want them to trust you and your brand.

Well, now it's your turn to get specific with what you want to share with the world. These four questions can help you think beyond the limits of generalizing, thus bringing out your true essence in your presence.

Write your answers on a fresh sheet of paper. Also, do keep a few more sheets of paper in case you want to refine your answers.

Q1. What industry, or huge topic, do you want to focus on? Why this industry? Get to the details of it. Some examples are Business growth, Personal development, Health & Wellness, Career growth, Arts & Craft, Business Management, etc.

Q2. What is your intention or goal that you want to achieve? It doesn't have to be monetary goals. It can be something related to the self-development of a person or something specific in terms of numbers or targets. For example, reputation, success, growth, high income, better work-life balance, a particular strategy, confidence, etc.

Q3. What topic would you choose in the vast topic or industry you have chosen? Could it be Yoga in Health & Wellness, Business automation in Business growth, or Leadership in Career growth or Personal development? Be specific with this one.

Q4. What would you want to be known for in your topic of choice? Something that makes you stand out. For example, in Yoga, you have vinyasa yoga, ashtanga yoga, or wheel yoga. In Leadership, you have leader mindset development, team leadership, corporate leadership, etc.

Answer each of these questions in detail. The key is to be really specific with your words.

Don't do this once. Do it at least three or four times and see how your message starts developing.

Bringing meaning to your message will always take time. If it didn't, then be sure that you haven't put much thought into it. It's okay to take time in developing a simple message that you stand by. But if you're taking time to build a message that is not specific, then you're wasting your time.

Write down your 'DIVE' at least three times. Refine it until you are sure about it.

INTERVIEW DIARIES

What is your take on niching it down when it comes to becoming a solution to one's problems?

For me, it's always the story. God's given you some sort of tragedy in your life, which you overcome—that's your niche. This is debatable, but I believe in this approach. What have you overcome in life that you have a solution to? That's your niche. When it's so personal to you, you understand everything about it!

You are an expert at it without ever studying it because you managed to overcome it. So that, to me, is the strongest niche! Either your research or your results should decide your niche. If you can marry the two, then that's what you call a role model. The combination, to me, is the ultimate!

– Puja Puneet, Life Coach, Author, and CEO of *Life By Design*

6

EXPERIENCE + RELEVANCE = STORIES

The most powerful person in the world is a Storyteller

– Steve Jobs

Take yourself back to your childhood days and think about that golden question that your parents asked you: "What do you want to become when you grow up?" What would your answer be?

A one-word answer, or you would actually talk about it like this.

"When I grow up, I want to become a pilot so that I can take my family on a nice long vacation to Spain and then when we are there we will explore all the cities, eat good food, visit the museums and then come back home." How innocent does that sound?

Now imagine the impact you can have today through your passionate story. You express it in the same way, innocently and with conviction.

Here's the secret.

We are already telling stories as we live each day.

We tell stories from the time we start talking.

We tell stories about things that happen around us.

We tell stories about dreams and nightmares.

We even tell stories about how we do things every single day.

Innocently.

Passionately.

And with so much excitement.

That is our human tendency.

We're told stories, and then we tell stories. Not only through what we see every day but also through what we create.

And when we create something, it is our own masterpiece that helps us tell a story so passionately because it's what we visualized and put on paper.

Now think about your brand, your message, or how you plan to help people in your life. You're the creator of this concept. How will you tell your story?

Ever since I understood that I could express myself, I knew I enjoyed telling stories. There was a point during my school days when I used to hesitate with uncertainty when I had to explain what happened just a while ago, but I would still say it in my own way. It was a nerve-wracking experience for me. But today, when I look back, I thank myself for not giving up and just constantly working on it.

But that is really the beauty of storytelling—you say it in your own way, and then you keep refining it and changing it so that it sounds better than the previous version!

An idea or concept becomes a force of imagination when you create a story around it. Why do you think stories are told to children? Nowadays, the education system has changed in so many ways, and a boring math calculation is taught using a story so that kids grasp it easily. Lucky kids! We were told old stories of a woman stuck in a tower, with her long hair used as a ladder, or another woman losing her glass slipper.

Were they interesting? Of course! Why? Because it stimulated our imaginations. It created stories in our minds. Maybe they weren't stories that 'taught' us something, but they were ways to help us think beyond a certain point.

Now, if you make sense of your own brand story and make people visualize where they can be after they invest in your concept, wouldn't that be magical?

If a story is captivating, it can really do the trick. And that's why it's so important when building a brand presence. It's what increases the grasping power of us impatient human beings who have a really short attention span. The days of long, boring, and tiring training are over. Be it in school, college, or even online learning, it has all taken a different route, a route that involves experiences, stories, and uplifting of emotions. People want to be on their toes, constantly doing something.

Even the certified couch potatoes want something that could captivate their attention. Trust me when I say that they want to experience something they can learn from.

Your story is a unique aspect of how you portray your brand presence. If it's strong, it will move your audience.

Remember what Steve Jobs said: "If you're a storyteller, you're powerful!"

Words play a powerful role in convincing people. The emotions that come out from the way you put it together make one take action.

This is something I experienced and realized very late in my training and coaching career. When I first started out, it was only about 'introducing yourself' followed by 'training content,' which any normal trainer would go about doing.

The spice of experiences was never really encouraged because "Hello! I had no idea!"

Often, my training would go fairly well. But beyond a point, it got extremely tedious and monotonous. There was something missing. That extra 'masala' was not there, and I often wondered what on earth was I missing out on.

Fast forward to 2017. Oh, yes! You would've realized that this year did A LOT to me. But anyway, this was the year I decided that I needed to up my game in training and coaching, not because I was bad at it, but because I genuinely got bored of it. So I started loosening up at my training and speaking assignments by watching and learning from TED Talks, YouTube videos, and books.

I realized that the spark comes out when an experience is narrated, and that's when I found the masala that I had to add. It was so simple. My own story!

In my next training, at a popular IT company, on branding yourself, I started off like this.

"How many of you want to become successful in your job?"

"How many of you want to know how I did it?"

A lot of buzzes, a lot of YESes came my way, and I told them my story just like I'm telling you my stories in this book.

We're told to follow a certain way, a certain strategy, a certain thought process that allows us to think in a certain way. We're also conditioned to behave, act, and do in a certain way. In every industry, there are rules. But that doesn't mean we become robots of the industry, right?

What really makes *you* stand out from the noise? You might be great at what you do. You might have years of experience. But it doesn't stop at the years of experience you have.

The question is, what do you have that no one else in your industry has? Your own set of experiences that set your values and beliefs. That sets you apart from the rest. Your own story!

Now think about your topic. The topic you chose in the previous chapter through 'DIVE' strategy. How would you help your audience connect with what you're offering? You plug in your experiences with the goal that you're trying to achieve.

Imagine you're being interviewed and asked the following questions:

What got you here?

What made you realize that this is your calling?

How can you help?

Why do you want to help?

What problem are you solving?

Who needs to hear your story? What was your breakthrough?

What challenges did you face? What is your mission?

Now while reading, you would have formed rough answers to all these questions because you already have them ready, not because you saw this coming, but because you've experienced it before.

If you put these answers into one paragraph and format it, keeping the sequence in mind, you'll have a natural story that you can tell anyone at any time.

I always believe that the power to create, express, and build lies within us. We just need to tap into that power to nurture it. Your story is your form of self-expression, and that's what helps you stand out from the noise around you. The secret to a good story is the ability to create a strong connection with your audience.

And when you do that, you become a natural force of radiating energy that makes them want to listen to you further. You might make mistakes, pronounce differently, or express yourself in your local language, or not even use as many words and still form a permanent image of a prominent leader in the eyes of your audience.

Now think about your topic again. Write down the following details that together become the framework of your story that you can use permanently.

Write down five turning points in your life. It can be anything big or small. What were those moments that changed the game for you?

Write down the challenges that you faced on the way. What were those roadblocks that tried to stop you from achieving your goals, but you overcame them anyway?

Write down three role models in your life who have guided you in your journey so far. For example, your parents, your grandparents, your teacher, your coach, your friend, a stranger, or anyone else.

Write down three skills that were once your weaknesses but now have become your strengths because you worked on them or something happened, and it changed you for good.

Close your eyes and visualize how you want people to see you. What should they know you for, and why should they know you and the work you do?

If you were invited to talk about what you do, how would you begin? Create three versions of your beginning.

Whatever you just wrote are signals or cues that can be used in your story, and nothing can be more original than these answers. Don't overthink each answer. Just go with the flow and answer each question like it's a rapid-fire round. The answers that first come to your mind are probably what you need to share with your audience in your next story.

INTERVIEW DIARIES

How does one sound relatable when they are building a brand story?

Facts tell, stories sell, and a story is what connects with the audience. But having shared that, my mentor says that when you're going through a tough situation, don't share that story at that moment. You share your story after you've been through it and passed on from the situation. Whether it is a story of flunking your exams, losing your job, or having a breakdown, it's something that has happened, you found a solution to, and not facing that situation anymore. Your story becomes a lesson that others can learn from.

Another thing about stories is that the more vulnerable you are, the more trust you can build. Most people show their good side but hesitate to show their flaws. But when you are transparent about what you share, people get attracted to you and start relating with you.

Everybody wants to build trust by showing what they have done. But, for me, it's the other way round. Most people don't get it. Many marketers do it by flashing their cars and 'showing' what they got, which works for them. The fact is that their vibe attracts their tribe. But over a period of time, people get smarter and know that it's just a show-off.

When it comes to human-to-human connection, they see the vulnerability and understand the person is genuinely there to help them."

– Siddharth Rajsekar, India's leading Digital Coach & Lifestyle Entrepreneur

7

PRODUCTIVITY + PROGRESSION - PERFECTION = PRO-POSITION!

Progress is impossible without change, and those who cannot change their minds cannot change anything

– George Bernard Shaw

Back in the day, as an aspiring entrepreneur with big dreams, there was this one big stigma that stopped me from thinking beyond the invisible line of comfort. I call it the Perfection Stigma. I always believed that to be successful in my journey, I got to be perfect at every single thing I did. So I got on this long trip of learning from various people, reading self-help and business books, and figuring out ways to build my brand presence by learning and implementing things. I had so many beliefs around entrepreneurship that today, I wonder if I really am on edu-steroids? Just kidding!

The biggest insecurity that drove me to educate myself about things I wasn't taught in school was that I had zero experience in marketing and business management. I didn't know how to build a business, and I was under this perception that the 'content' had to be perfect before I shared it with the world. By content, I mean skills, topics, and everything else that I had got 'certified' in. There was no such thing as 'market yourself' or 'position yourself' in my dictionary. What I understood was, as a trainer, I had to train people on topics that I was qualified to teach.

That's it. I didn't think of putting my message out there, nor did I feel the need to tell people that this is what I do and am good at. Why?

Because I wanted to first be perfect at what I did.

It looked 'unethical' to market myself without being certified.

The business was not for me.

Today, I look back at these three beliefs, and I slap my big palm on my forehead.

What was I thinking?

But that's what the truth is. In our journey towards making a name, our beliefs are created around what people tell us, what we see around us, and how we're convinced about what we experience and who we are. Nobody tells you that taking a risk is alright, and only if you try will you know if it works or doesn't. Only after the change in business trends and how people see success have we realized that it is okay to take the leap of faith.

But this leads us to be insecure, and when we are actually good at things we thought we weren't, we doubt ourselves, which kills our scope of creativity. It's such a sad state of affairs; the power of influence and conditioning is so strong that we mature too early in life, neglecting the raw, natural ways of thinking that truly define us.

It took me some time to figure out that it's alright to be good at things that I thought I wasn't and that my existence is really about learning on the go and sharpening those skills to create a better version of myself than I was yesterday.

In my early days, as a coach and trainer, many people would tell me, "Diya, why don't you start sharing your content online? Let them know how good you are."

And here's what my 'lethal' answer was: "Oh! I hate marketing and talking about myself online! It'll look like I'm showing off my skills, and

I don't want people talking behind my back." My answer would get me rolling eyes and pitiful nods and answers like this one: "Sigh! Up to you. You don't know what you're missing."

But as and when the years passed, I started realizing that the competition is getting more intense, and people are doing all kinds of things to brand themselves better.

It started feeling more like a race and less like a journey. And here's something I figured out while watching all these runners head in a certain direction. There are two kinds of winners: the Robots and the Stars.

The robot is the one who does the drill, follows, and moves on while being programmed to think and believe in a certain way. Whereas the star is the one who takes the road less travelled, explores new ways, fails, follows certain strategies, and then eventually stands out in the industry. Both are winners but with different results.

I could relate a lot with the 'Star'; this is what woke me up and made me realize that I could create things beyond the ordinary. I decided to explore things that weren't in my comfort zone, in my brand building. What do you think was the first thing I worked on?

It was marketing.

I started sharing content online, interacting with people, and posting stories about myself. Then I tried out various systems to see what works best for me and what kind of marketing is my business's calling. While experimenting, I subconsciously positioned myself as a leader because people started interacting with me and asking me questions related to my industry.

Oh, and this time, I got more rolling eyes and pitiful nods from a small bunch of people that are always there to criticize your work—the naysayers. That's the gift you get so that you keep progressing in what you do.

At first, it took me a while to accept this 'gift,' but I soon took this on as something that allowed me to start thinking creatively.

It's true that when you're on your way to positioning yourself by showing people what you do, there are a lot of them who would like what you do or otherwise. While developing your positioning in the industry, you also need to grow a thick skin to protect yourself from the naysayers.

But then there are also times when you give up, and your fears start taking over. That's what happened to me while I was working on many aspects of my presence. I had phased out of insecurity, but then slowly, the 'imposter syndrome' crept in.

I would question myself so many times before actually putting out content online.

"Will they resonate with this?"

"Do I sound good?"

"Do I look fine?"

"Can I call myself an expert in this field?" and more thoughts on similar lines.

I did get a lot of naysayers telling me that I'm not cut-out for this, but instead of letting that pull me down, I gained more confidence and worked on it.

The more comments and feedback I got, the more I progressed and refined my presence as a coach in the industry. It was literally like building a monument that needed a strong foundation that was difficult to pull down. And that, my friend, made my naysayers burn big time while watching me grow.

I went on a trip of building self-confidence in videos, besides sharpening my presence online. There were so many first-time moments on the way, but in the end, those were the most exciting because there was no room for mundane work. There was room only for creation and progression.

The real secret to being outstanding in what you do is to be progressively and intentionally involved in the journey that you have chosen. The way Tony Robbins says it: "Life feels like it is happening TO you when actually life is happening FOR you." Designing the way it unfolds is in our hands. You reading this book didn't happen by fluke; you made it happen. Each experience, good or bad, is a gift that shows you the way.

That's why I strongly believe in the power of 'Pro-Positioning,' wherein I work on being extremely productive by progressing in every single thing I do, without aiming for perfection.

There is no room for perfection if you want to 'Pro-Position' yourself. What I mean by pro-position is to become 'The Star' of your industry. Do things that few people do: take the challenging route, explore the unexplored, create a mess and then fix it, and try not to follow the crowd. But then, be smart and focus on what really works for you (if you know what I mean).

Boil it down to simplifying your approach so that you have a clear path towards amplifying your reputation.

Whenever you're introduced to a new system or strategy, you need to give it your 100%. But after that, there are going to be some changes that YOU make so that it works for you. This stands valid only and only when you have tried something and decided on if it works for you. This doesn't mean that the strategy or system didn't work for you. It just means that you followed somebody else's journey, trying to figure out your own on the way while allowing yourself to progress in a direction that works best for you.

In other words, you're *pro-positioning* yourself by adding quality experiences, education, and productivity into your journey.

There are three very important 'pro' traits of a Pro-Position leader: progression, productivity, and professionalism. If there is a green tick near each trait, you're already successful in building your own presence as an expert in your industry.

Now, here's a question for you. Do you want to amplify your reputation as a Pro-Position Leader in your industry?

Then you got to friend your fears and break your barriers and make things happen *for* you. There is a reason why things are the way they are right now.

Take a look around you. Where are you sitting? What are you doing? What are you wearing? Look at every single part of your current surroundings. You have made it happen for yourself.

So if you want to Pro-Position yourself in the industry, you have to create your own world of progression and success. If you leave it the way it is, you can very well join the Robot Bandwagon!

My writing this book is something that I made happen. I wanted you to read it. And by the way, this is my very first book, but nothing stopped me. I don't have to be an established author to write a book about the way I designed my personal brand presence.

Nobody is perfect. I am not; you're not. And that's what actually makes us successful.

If success was all about 'perfection,' then where is all the fun that makes it a memorable journey. What will you tell the people you want to inspire?

Would you tell them, "The journey was perfect, and I am successful" or "The journey is a story worth telling, and all those memorable experiences got me where I am today"?

Here's something you need to do before you head to the next chapter.

Vision yourself having achieved a goal. This could be any goal, big or small, that you have been wanting to accomplish.

Write down the following.

Let's assume that you have achieved the goal that you have in mind. Take a notepad and write it down. For example, I have finally launched my book on Amazon, and it's already doing so well!

Write down five or six big steps that helped you achieve this goal. For example, 1. Outline of my book; 2. Manuscript completion; 3. Editing; 4. Publishing; 5. Marketing.

Now think of how you approach each step towards the big steps mentioned in the previous point. For example, book outline. 1. What topic am I covering? 2. Who will read this book? 3. What should be the theme? 4. How many chapters roughly? 5. What should be the reader's journey while reading this book? 6. What is the goal?

After completing the above three steps, think of how to schedule the mini-steps to achieve the first big step. For example, the mini-steps to the first big step won't take more than a day or two to complete. Schedule that accordingly.

Write down a deadline that you give yourself for achieving each step. For example, the outline of my book—1 week.

If you approach each goal this way, you will find yourself becoming more productive, progressive, and, most definitely, better positioned than many other players in your industry.

INTERVIEW DIARIES

Every entrepreneur wants to stand out in their industry. Do share your perspective on positioning oneself in the industry.

If you look at the internet and how it's going right now, there are a lot of people doing similar things. But what has worked for me in the last twenty-seven months of being in the trenches of doing this business on a daily basis is a unique representation of concepts. For example, if I'm learning from three to four different mentors, I integrate all that knowledge. And by the way, I present it in my videos and podcasts, and it comes from my own head and forms my version of it. This means that I use a clean sheet of paper, and I put those points down based on my understanding and interpretation of what I learned.

For example, Jack Canfield's *The Success Principles* is built from *Law of Success* by Napoleon Hill. It is his take on the topic in his style, his version, and his interpretation.

The fact is that there is no information that is new. But what can be unique is the representation of that information. Even though there is coaching, affiliate marketing, products, etc., in my business, I have represented them in my unique way, and that is the Freedom Business Model, which has become a buzzword nowadays.

– Siddharth Rajsekar, India's leading Digital Coach & Lifestyle Entrepreneur

8

MARKETING TALKS, STORY SELLS

Marketing is no longer about the stuff that you make but about the stories that you tell

— Seth Godin

My journey towards becoming a business creator had a very rocky start, and it didn't look very promising, to begin with. Before I could even think of how to go about it, I fell into the trap of limiting beliefs that would make me think that I wasn't cut-out for this. One of the strongest ones was that of marketing, and that it really wasn't for me as I didn't have a degree to pursue it. That was a harmful drug for my growth mindset. I was willing to take the leap of faith but would end up stopping because I thought I wasn't good enough to do things that were challenging.

Now, here's the truth about being your own boss.

As you grow and build your own presence, you're going to have a stream of thoughts and beliefs visiting you every now and then. Call them your 'mind friends' who will try to guide you, advise you, and stop you from doing a few things.

Now, who are these 'mind friends'?

They are the guys who would tell you *not* to step out of your comfort zone and put your skin in the game.

They are the guys who will make you trust them first and then hypnotize you to not do what you want to do.

The biggest mistake I made was following those 'mind friends' at the wrong times. I kept nurturing those friendships until it led me to believe that I was fine where I was, not having the required skills to grow a business because one of my mind friends told me that it was a big risk to take and that being where I was was just right.

You can call it ignorance, but I did find it blissful and convenient at that moment, as very often, I would believe that staying comfortable in my own zone was the right way to build a brand.

What did this lead to?

I lagged in building my brand.

Competition got ahead of me.

My urge for learning a new skill faded away.

And the growth mindset ended up being a stagnant space of skills, knowledge, and ideas.

I am sure you wouldn't want to become stagnant in your growth!

The secret we all know is that the ability to grow and build ourselves in the way we want majorly depends on us. It is about how we take things further and make them happen for ourselves.

The human mind is constantly conditioned by what people say to you and what you believe. Breaking out of those thoughts and beliefs and actually going on a journey that you wish to make is something you have right now, but are you willing to make use of it?

Here's what I did.

Now, when I started 'unfollowing' my mind friends through a constant battle and focused more on things that I needed to concentrate on, I started seeing myself grow beyond my own limiting thoughts and beliefs.

And to my surprise, what I despised the most, ended up being something I enjoyed exploring.

Content marketing!

I realized that content marketing was really for me! I started exploring marketing for my own presence, and it became a fun tool for me to play with, besides helping me stand out from the noise in my industry. I started loving the idea of expressing myself in my own unique way. It was the noise that I had to create to stand out from the noise.

That 'noise' is not about being a preacher, but being a teacher that would show the way through her experiences. And hello, that's why I'm writing this book.

That noise is the story.

I realized one thing for sure. People don't care about how good you are at marketing. But as long as you have a genuine story to tell, they WILL most definitely want to associate themselves with you.

Think about your own behaviour when it comes to checking out a product or service you might be interested in. You are curious to know more about it, but when you see that it doesn't have a high relatability factor in the words that have been used to convince you about how beneficial it is, you tend to lose interest.

But if it's the same product or service that shows you the story while taking you through a journey along with a sense of relatability, it will most definitely pull you towards it because you found it interesting and probably saw yourself in that story.

Now think about your potential customers.

Do you want them to relate to your story, or do you want them to consider you as just another service or product that can be considered some other time?

If you want them to take action *now*, you have to make a story out of your offer. And when you do that, you're making noise that's worth listening.

You don't want them to shut your noise down because they didn't connect with you. What really helps them connect with you and what you have to offer is the value that you are sharing. Many times we tend to think that giving out more than we should is not good. But if you don't, how do you expect them to believe in what you are offering?

The two biggest traits that you can leverage in marketing are:

1. Vulnerability

2. Transparency

It isn't always about your accomplishments or credibility. People honestly want you to feel how they feel when it comes to any challenge they are facing. You might have years of experience in a particular skill, but if that doesn't solve a problem that your audience is facing, that experience doesn't stand valid for them. When you show your vulnerable side, you're directly showing empathy, which makes you a leader that they can follow and trust. Let's be honest. You have been there too! You have struggled on the way, had your own set of challenges, failed a few times, and then figured out ways to stand up on your feet.

So, as a personal brand online or offline, you are showcasing your presence as a cumulative result of what you have experienced. And when you share it with your audience, they appreciate it and feel comfortable listening to your story.

I always believe that marketing only tells people what, why, and how of a product or service, but a story sells what, why, and how of the same. Thousands of people are creating concepts, products, ideas, services, and systems every single day.

You're just a molecule in all that noise. You will continue to be a molecule if you don't express yourself and be authentic in your approach.

The way you market yourself through your story can help you amplify the size of your own existence in the industry.

When I launched my brand, Design Your Presence™, in 2019, even though it was an extension of what I was already doing, it made so much more sense when I started talking about it. People saw the true essence of my presence and understood what I was really offering.

I also saw a lot of coaches and trainers copying the concept in their own ways. But instead of confronting them about it, I took it as a compliment and went ahead and trademarked "Design Your Presence™".

Why didn't I do this earlier?! Well, I guess there is a time for everything.

The focus is really on making it simple to understand, easy to relate to, and definitely unique.

Building my marketing voice was by far the most important part of my presence. It challenged me to think out of the box and come up with creative concepts to help people grasp concepts with ease.

I even launched a six-step strategy that you would have noticed through this book. It is called the S.T.A.R Strategy, and it stands for 'Simplify to Amplify Reputation.' I focus on six key areas to build a brand presence online: specificity, story, positioning, online presence, thoughtful marketing, and finally, of course, reputation!

When a concept makes sense to you, it most definitely will make sense to others around you. But it doesn't stop there. The practicality of what you offer has to be something that you have tried and tested before and have actually developed results for yourself. People always think about how this is going to benefit them first. So, to validate the workability of your offer, things like social proof and case studies work.

Remember when you started out? Maybe you learned something from someone, got coached or mentored by someone, or even made that someone your go-to expert for any questions related to the subject. Whatever it might be, you wanted to see results. You wanted to get the most out of that 'someone' because it was really about you in this case. That 'someone' told you a story of their own experience, which drove you to believe in them further.

That story made you take action.

That story made you say these words in your mind: "I'm sold!"

Marketing can be a really tricky part of how you portray your presence in the industry, and to stand out, the only way to be different and to think differently is to 'create' something that works for you and your audience.

Now, it's action time.

Think of what you plan to market in the next seven days. This could be a programme, a service, a system, a fan page, a masterclass, anything. Think about how you are going to create your "I'm sold!" story. Here are a few points to consider in terms of the framework.

Start with a question or fact related to the problem you are solving.

Start the story with "Back in 2007, when I was in school…"

Share the experience.

Then talk about what you learned.

Talk about what you achieved.

This then ends with the solution to the problem you are solving!

End with a call-to-action!

And voila! You have a story that sells.

INTERVIEW DIARIES

The truth is that great marketing is the need of the hour for any business. What makes an entrepreneur a hygienic and overall great marketer?

When I work with entrepreneurs, especially new entrepreneurs, I tell them that they need to have some kind of proactive and consistent effort to market themselves. It could be social media, joining a referral network like BNI, participating in exhibitions, listing yourself on search engines like Justdial or Google search or whatever. I believe that every entrepreneur needs to take consistent and proactive action in the ACTIVITY of marketing. Otherwise, your business runs on word-of-mouth. And when your business depends on word-of-mouth, it's great, but it works like a bonus. It means that you're doing great work, and certain people are willing to trust you with their family and friends. But through this, you cannot control the leads you generate on a weekly or monthly basis. You cannot predict what would be the enquiry generation of your business. So, marketing is a foundational activity for any entrepreneur. Having said that, a lot of entrepreneurs misunderstand the difference between marketing and advertising. For me, marketing is more about adding value and engaging with people, whereas advertising is self-promotion. I see a lot of people go and advertise themselves and say, "This is me. This is who I am. This is my product or service." But they don't focus on sharing value with people. Now, based on your business, you need to look at if education is the right method of marketing. Building online content, videos, podcasts, etc., is one marketing strategy. The other theme can be entertainment. Can entertaining your clients be a marketing strategy? If you're a coffee shop owner, then what can you do in an event wherein people experience the place.

So marketing is all about value addition. It is about how you showcase your expertise and engage your client in a manner where they trust you, like you, respect you, and want to enquire from you. I feel every entrepreneur needs to figure their own channel out. It's not a 'one size fits all' game.

– Rajiv Talreja, India's leading Business Coach, best-selling author of Lead or Bleed

According to you, what are the top marketing strategies that work well in today's changing times?

So, if I had to break that down, Diya, I would rather give the people three questions to answer. Because based on those three questions, they'll know how to market changes. The first question is: "Who is your target customer?" You got to break down from a demographic as well as a psychographic point of view. What is their age, gender, profession, occupation, etc.? Because if you think everybody is your customer, then nobody is your customer. And in that segment, who has the money, who has the authority and need. Because if you are offering your products or services to someone who doesn't have money, you'll obviously end up singing the song "I don't have money," and you'll lose confidence in your own product or service. So, you need to understand who has the money, who has the authority to make a decision, and who has the need for your product or service.

Once you know *who* your customer is, you then need to know what *channel* is your customer on. Is your customer available on Facebook or Instagram or YouTube or LinkedIn, or is he/she available on WhatsApp? Or is your customer not available on any of these platforms and is available in an apartment complex nearby or even a school/college or academic institution or a particular industrial body or association or business network? You really need to know what is the right channel.

With social media and digital media picking up, a lot of people, even though their business doesn't need social media, because of the 'fear of missing out,' are spending money on learning digital marketing, giving projects to agency managers to handle their digital marketing accounts, but it's leading to nothing! They get ten-thousand likes by doing a paid campaign, and then they have "Too Cool Rahul" and "Sexy Salma" liking their pages. That is not your audience!

The truth is you need to know where your customer is available.

This brings me to the next thing, which is *content*. What will suit my product or service and my customer's liking and interest? Will it be education or entertainment or some kind of engagement? Will it be videos or webinars, YouTube channels, podcast shows, interviews, blog articles? Will it be infographics? Will it be partnering with influencers? I think marketing is a science of these three C's—Customer, Channel, and Content. You need to see what adds value to your audience.

– Rajiv Talreja, India's leading Business Coach,
best-selling author of *Lead or Bleed*

9
ONE, TWO, THREE, AND ACTION!

You may never know what results come from your action.
But if you do nothing, there will be no result

— Mohandas Karamchand Gandhi

The journey of any business starts and continues with just one thing—constant action. Now, while reading this, you might say, "Yes, Diya, we already know this." But what we also know is that 95% of entrepreneurs stop at just knowing and not doing anything about it.

The fact is that if you really want to see the results, you have to do the work! Whoever said that things will "happen" to you when they have to has clearly guided you wrong. When you look at any brand or business around you, you might just see the finished product because that's what they want you to see.

Did the final outcome happen overnight? Absolutely not!

It took them multiple failures, hours of brainstorming, tons of research, months or years of refining, and more things that got them to design and construct something so amazing that is the finished product or service.

The truth is they took action and 'made it happen' for themselves.

Now, you might say that those are 'company brands' and not personal brands. Yes! But the fact is that this applies to even someone who is working as a solopreneur. Your personal brand presence precedes your company brand because people need to connect with you to understand the product or service better. To make any brand work, the human mind behind it needs to design, draft, and deliver the result, and that gets more convincing when the human mind is the brand in itself.

Your existence as a brand speaks loud about the outcomes you could give your audience, and the highest contributing element to construct this path to the finish line is your mind.

I have had tons of phases in my journey wherein I had to think ten times before taking action. And what would stop me? The two questions: "What will people say?" and "Will they like the idea?"

Remember we spoke about 'mind friends' in the previous chapter?

They will always try to keep you in your comfort zone unless you start breaking away from those limiting beliefs and think beyond your own boundaries.

The day I started realizing that the only way to scale up what I am doing was to take action, I started seeing results in no time. The results can look like these:

An evident rise in your income.

A growing community of loyal followers.

A positive change in your own mindset.

An improvement in your skillset.

A growing presence on social media.

A higher recognition for the work you do.

And the list goes on…

I have always been an anxious person right from childhood. Reasons? From the time I started understanding things like peer pressure and teacher expectations in school, I have constantly been of the opinion that I'm not good enough and that I need to keep working on myself. And if I don't, it won't be good for me. So, to consciously work on those thoughts, I had to build myself in such a way that there was no room for any kind of pressure or expectation.

One thing led to another, and I realized that in every area of my life, I had to build my presence in such a way that would allow me to break the barriers towards any kind of growth I wanted to experience.

Whether it was working after marriage, building my business, or experiencing things I thought I couldn't.

That drive is one of the reasons why I take action in every single aspect of my business. After all, if you're building something masterful, don't you have to be the master at it?

Here's another truth about designing your presence. Every brand or business survives on change.

Change of plan

Change of strategy

Change of ideas

Change of thoughts

Change of mind

Change of perspective

Change of literally *everything*.

And that can happen when you decide to stop believing in things that limit you and start taking action towards growing in every aspect of your brand building.

Just like in making a movie, there are thousands of takes, and then, finally, something clicks. As I write this book, I still explore new things for my brand presence, try out different approaches towards content creation, figure out another way to sell my services, and whatnot. I do it every day, and while at it, the learning happens on the go.

It's a journey that you constantly mould.

Think about the big names in the industry who are where they are today because of the action they took, even when they didn't have to. As entrepreneurs, we are going to reach a point when we are doing fine and don't need to do anything more to grow our presence. That is the most dangerous mindset for your business growth.

Even when you're comfortable, if you have the urge to grow the business and presence consistently, you have to be okay to do things that aren't required at that moment for you to stay in the game.

Somewhere around the end of the year 2017, I was at my lowest in terms of income. Of course, after you are fired from your lucrative job and have to start over, it can be quite a choppy ride against the waves! So, during this time, one of the nights, I got this idea out of the blue to become a fitness instructor.

Here's something about me. I get some of the weirdest, craziest, and sometimes the most amazing ideas before I'm just about to sleep.

So it didn't stop at being a fitness instructor. I also wanted to learn Art Therapy so that I could convert my art (I'm an artist as well on the side) into therapeutic sessions to relieve stress.

Both sounded like great ideas for 'passive income.' I was so proud of myself as both the ideas revolved around my talents.

So, I found the training to become a Zumba instructor. It so happened that the next training was in a week. And so I geared up for my training and went and got myself certified in no time.

And then, a few days after that, I found an online course on Art Therapy.

I paid for both the training and felt great at that moment.

Now here's what happened. I didn't do well as a Zumba instructor, even though I have been a great dancer all my life, nor did I pursue Art Therapy because, for that, you need a degree or some qualification to become an official therapist. And I had no intention to study for another few years to go in that direction.

You'll probably ask me, then why did you waste the money and do those courses?

My answer is, learning is never a waste of time or money. What if I hadn't explored these two fields on the way? To this very day, I would be thinking about exploring them to see what was in store for me.

I did make a small income through Zumba. I even became an AFAA-certified group fitness instructor. Oh, and I also took up a new group fitness certification called Pound Fitness, a cardio-based workout inspired by drumming.

It sounded fun, so I explored it.

The reason I am telling you this is even though I've been a trainer and coach since 2011, I tried everything on the way so that I know what my true calling was. Celebrity styling, a full-time job, corporate training, image consulting, fitness, art therapy, canvas art, textiles, and a few more.

At every step, whether it was joining a company full-time or doing an online course, or taking a detour and exploring another industry like fitness, it contributed to my experience and advancement towards building my presence, which got me to where I am today.

I got a lot of friends and family who asked me why and how I am doing so many things. But that's what you need to do before singularly focusing on one thing that is your core purpose.

When it comes to the results, of course, none of these ideas worked in my favour. At first, I did feel like it was a waste of time, energy, and money. But the result was my own doing because, in the back of my mind, my focus was on training and coaching people in building their own brands, and that's why Design Your Presence™ is where it is today—growing, changing, and creating.

I launched Design Your Presence™ after many takes, many ideas, and many discussions around how I wanted to be seen in front of people. It really is about how you make things happen so that it works in your favour.

Nobody has the right to make you believe in things that they believe in. The only person who can convince you how you want and need to be is you. We all make mistakes, take risks, fail, and stand up again. That is a part of the deal, right?

Now, coming to making you take action.

Write down your very next three actions that you plan to take in the next week. They don't have to be big. They can be small actions that can change the game of your business and brand presence.

Next, have a mini-game plan for each action. What are you going to do in order to get this action done?

For example, ACTION: I will get my logo/brand name design. MINI GAME PLAN: 1. Think of what I want to get done; 2. Look for inspiration on Pinterest; 3. Write down in brief what I am looking for in the logo (design, colours, feel/mood, industry, etc.); 4. Find a designer on Fiverr; 5. Get the job done!

And finally, just get it done. Don't sit on it. You may think that this is not the right time, the right place, the right action to take, or whatever you have on your mind. Don't let those thoughts stop you. Just go, take action.

Success is waiting for you!

INTERVIEW DIARIES

What is the advice you can give a new entrepreneur, coach, or trainer when it comes to taking action and getting work done?

I think the perspective missing largely in entrepreneurs, coaches, or trainers who are creating content on social media, or entrepreneurs looking to build a personal brand, is that they are looking at doing marketing more as a need to get a certain number of leads. That paradigm worked three years back. Today, that doesn't work. If you got to do marketing, you just get to it as a part of an everyday routine of growing your brand. Because if you're not marketing, you have no social assets, no social media presence, and nobody knows who you are. So you got to do marketing for the sake of doing marketing. You may be doing videos on LinkedIn, for example, but you might not be getting enquiries from those videos. But tomorrow, if you are sitting face-to-face with a corporate client and pitching yourself, that client would like to go back and refer to some of your videos, or you would want to send a couple of links to your clients, saying, "Hey, check out my latest profile or channel. I share a lot of content on the relevant topic." So it's not necessary that the content you put out there will give you a result immediately. It's like building social assets. And if you don't build those social assets today, then here's what will happen—you'll be that person who missed out on the 'real estate boom.' You know there was a generation in the 1990s that invested in real estate, and then there was another generation that thought, "Oh, this place is so far. Who will buy a plot over there?" Today, they take their kids to those localities and say, "Child, I saw this house in 1990. It was offered for Rs. 3,00,000. Today, it costs around 5 crores (50 million)." The son then wonders what pathetic financial decisions they'd made. You don't want your children to say that about your social media tomorrow. You *need* to build those assets today! Often, I hear entrepreneurs say that it's too late to start. I say it's late to start, but do you want to delay it further and make it much later, or you want to start now?

– Rajiv Talreja, India's leading Business Coach, best-selling author of *Lead Or Bleed*

10

DESIGN YOUR PRESENCE!

If your Presence doesn't make an impact,
your absence won't make a difference

– Unknown

Before I launched my brand and signature programme, Design Your Presence™, I was someone who had absolutely no intention to make it big online. I was always under the impression that meeting people face-to-face is more important than meeting them virtually. I really did not see the need to build my personal brand presence online as I was blindfolded with the belief that online wasn't for me and rebuilding what I had created would be too long a process.

My role as a freelance trainer and coach included a lot of travelling around the country. I used to love interacting with people, training employees and employers of some of the finest companies, and getting appreciated for the work I had been doing all those years. The money was there, and so was the appreciation. But what was missing was a sense of satisfaction post every training. I always felt that something more needed to be done. Something that would make me feel great about what I did. I was never elated by the outcome or by the effort I had put in.

Being a trainer and coach is extremely rewarding, especially when you're passionate about teaching people. That passion was there in me, for sure, but because I was on my own in the journey and didn't get the guidance that I required at that point, I started doubting myself.

They say that when you are alone, your thoughts take over you, and it is quite difficult to convince yourself that you're doing your bit.

To add to this, one of the things that didn't work in my favour most of the time was that age was not on my side. I was too young to be called a coach! I started training people in 2012 when I was 22 years old.

It was not until the end of 2018 that I realized that I was really good at what I did, and maybe I should dive deeper into it because I already had a presence designed as a knowledge-giver.

Fast forward to the second half of 2019. I visited a one-of-a-kind festival for trainers and coaches in a beautiful town of Mahabalipuram in Tamil Nadu called the 'Gamechangers Festival.'

It was hosted by Rajiv Talreja, one of the best business coaches in India, along with his team. I still don't know what got me to take the leap of faith and actually check it out, but it did me real good! It was during this festival that I realized what my strong purpose and true potential were, and what really was missing in my journey—*making my presence felt by many more people.*

After talking to other fellow trainers and coaches at the festival and sharing what I did and how I built my brand without any experience in technology, business, or marketing, I realized that I could help struggling entrepreneurs and knowledge-givers who aren't tech-savvy (just like me) in building an impactful brand presence online through online courses and coaching.

The only thing that I had to figure out was the medium through which I could do all this. This truly got me excited and geared up to revamp and rebuild my presence that was slowly growing towards saturation.

So, being someone who always wanted to be ahead in the game and just make things happen, I put on my *girl boss* crown and got cracking with it right away. I have always been of the opinion that if I can do it, anyone can.

This festival really changed the game for me! If it wasn't for a candid conversation with Rajiv on how to take things forward, I wouldn't be where I am today! I just wanted to get some clarity in building my brand as a trainer and coach, the way forward, what I should be doing and not doing, etc. At that moment, I was also oscillating between fitness & training and coaching. Though I was more inclined towards training people and wasn't really enjoying being a Zumba instructor, I needed some perspective from someone who had already been there. That brief five to ten-minute conversation got me to think beyond my little box of thoughts in my head. It was like a 'Get cracking' booster that I needed.

Rajiv told me to focus on two things: getting online to create an impact while focusing on coaching people one-on-one. The combination of both would set me on the path that would allow me to help a lot more people than I was already helping.

The truth is that I was one of the senior-most trainers at a prestigious institute, specializing in Image Consulting & Soft Skills Training. Though I would get a fair number of training assignments each month, it was not soul-satisfying at all. There were many factors that made it really monotonous for my growth, and that was one of the reasons why I had to see things differently.

Yes, I did fear going online and changing my strategy, but you got to do things that scare you so that you know how far you can go if you really have a strong mission to make a difference.

So, while Rajiv told me about this, I had a clouded mind with all kinds of 'rebranding' ideas springing up one after the other. My ideas started from merging fitness, personal branding, and soft skills with business branding to building an image. My mind faced a rapid-fire round of answers, and what came up first was building one's 'Presence.' Yup, back to realizing that 'presence' is the word that resonated with me the most for the longest time.

When he told me to try what he had said, I gave it a deep thought that evening and decided to step up my game and work on making my journey more fruitful and satisfying. So after getting back home, I got in touch with two amazing coaches to help me take things forward—Siddharth Rajsekar, a Digital Coach, and Puja Puneet, a Life Coach. Both of them helped me launch my brand, Design Your Presence™, the right way because they saw how strong my mission to help many entrepreneurs and knowledge-givers step up their game and build their brand presence in their own industry was.

Initially, it was quite a daunting task to learn and master digital. But an even bigger challenge was to get people to see me as an expert as I wasn't getting noticed online despite being in the industry for so long. Tables turned after I dived deep into learning, rewiring, and mastering tools, strategies, and systems. One thing led to another, and I got more confident at it, and while all that happened, Design Your Presence™ became a well-known brand and programme in just about a month! Something that I didn't expect? Yes, of course.

But getting online made me grow my business in just a few months!

Now I'm not advocating the whole idea of 'fast results' or 'get rich quick.' There is no such thing! But I got to build DYP™'s robust foundation in no time to see it constantly grow each day.

Why I'm sharing this with you? Because I know you can do it too. You can design your presence by being who you are without thinking that it's impossible. Whatever you create, whatever you do, people need to see you first and then your creation.

Though I have been focusing on Personal Branding offline, I realized that the scope is much more when you go online and set yourself apart as a prominent leader in your industry.

When I launched my first ever YouTube video, trust me, it was something that made me want to pull it down because it really wasn't great. I looked like an amateur, and it was so staged because I had spent six hours trying to perfect it. But that's something people don't really look at; they don't want to know how good you are with the backend stuff. They want to know what kind of value you can share with them authentically. And the value I shared in that video was something that got a lot of appreciation, which motivated me to create more videos still today.

Another factor that got me to design an impactful presence online was my belief that the 'number of followers or subscribers' is not important and that the number in my bank account is. And that change of mindset made things work faster for me. I wonder why entrepreneurs and knowledge-givers still believe that to influence others, they need a good following. When actually the truth is that it is your Presence, your value, your story that really pulls your audience towards you.

The days of 'vanity influence' are long gone. People observe what really works for them or what doesn't. The number game is a superficial way of showing fame, which lures you into believing that that's what your audience sees when actually it is *you* that they see.

Your presence is an evergreen source of influence online because people rely on consuming valid information from different parts of the world. So even a person living thousands of kilometres away from you can connect with you because they could relate to what you said in that post that they found either on your website, podcast, Instagram feed, or YouTube channel. Your presence can go viral in a matter of seconds if you do it right.

It really isn't about the number of years of experience either. I had to unlearn that thought in order to grow my presence online. Today, I confidently call myself 'An Eternal Learner,' learning new things every single day. When you set your intention to help more people through the knowledge you have, your potential to make a bigger impact increases a thousand-fold!

The very first thing that you need to think about is what kind of reputation you are building through your designed presence. How are people going to see you, and how will they relate to you and your mission? In the eyes of your audience, you need to be the leader they *choose* and not who they *know*.

INTERVIEW DIARIES

What is your take on the power of Reputation building?

I feel marketing is necessary for building that first impression.

Marketing is a door opener. When you market yourself well, it helps you open doors. Now once the door is opened, how well you do depends on your capabilities and your strengths, and you better be good at it. Otherwise, it can be equally brutal if you're not good at what you do and you are not marketing yourself. So, the stages of Reputation for me would be:

1. Create a Reach
2. Create A Result
3. Create A Recall

Marketing helps you build the reach first by opening the door to the right audience. Then, your product or service creates the result for your client, and that really earns you respect. The more you repeat the reach and result, the higher your recall becomes, and you become a brand!

So, I believe Reputation is these three stages. I also feel marketing and operations are like two legs, and they need to work in coordination. There are some people who are limping only in Operations, and they say, "I am good at what I do, and my work will speak for me." Well, there's too much noise in the world for your work to even be heard. So today, you got to speak for yourself besides your work speaking for you. Marketing and Operations are simultaneous processes that work towards building your Reputation.

– Rajiv Talreja, India's leading Business Coach, best-selling author of *Lead Or Bleed*

11

SIX INFLUENCE BUILDING MYTHS TO BUST

The only way on Earth to influence other people is to talk about what they want and show them how to get it

– Dale Carnegie

To wrap things up, I wanted to conclude this book with six Influence Building myths that you need to bust right away if you really want to design your presence the right way.

Myth No. 1

"People will buy my years of experience and knowledge. If I show them the facts, they will be influenced to take action."

Bust it. NOW.

The truth is people don't look at your years of experience and knowledge. Instead, they look at the quality and purpose behind what you share. What message are you sharing that is getting them to connect with you further? People believe in *connection*, and they really don't want to look at you as a search engine for information. If you focus on creating a nurturing relationship with them as a true leader, you become their selected leader, mentor, or coach whom they can trust.

Myth No. 2

"I need to have thousands of followers and subscribers before I can positively influence people."

Bust it. NOW.

The truth is that you need to first build your presence by focusing on what you are good at and what you want people to know you for. While you understand this, you also need to understand that you need to serve value so you can get a genuine following of people who would learn from you. You don't need thousands of followers who don't know you and what you offer; you need genuine followers who need your service/product so that they can reap the benefits from it. Vanity influence is your reputation at face value. Where the real business growth happens lies in the quality of your presence and what you share with your audience.

Myth No. 3

"I don't have the confidence to speak in front of a crowd. So I don't think I can build an influence."

Bust it. NOW.

In your journey towards building a successful brand presence, you will definitely come across skills that you *need* to master in order to make things work for you and your business. Just because you have never done it, it doesn't mean you can never do it. Building and mastering a skill takes practice, determination, and repetition. There's always a first time for everyone, and you can start by talking to a really small group of people. This will eventually increase your confidence, and as you see that happen, your size of the audience will increase. In no time, you will be more confident in sharing your stories, which could have a massive impact and influence.

Myth No. 4

"I don't know what to share with my audience. I don't have a valid story to tell."

Bust it. NOW.

The fact is that everyone has a valid story to tell. If you have lived this far, you will have at least three stories to tell your audience. There is a reason why you got here. There is a reason why you're doing something in a certain way. Maybe you want to help people because of a certain experience you had. Any story is good if it's valid and has a reason as to why you want to help your audience. Your story, big or small, can inspire many people to change their lifestyle, business, relationships, situation positively. The validity of your story becomes stronger when people see you as someone who experienced it and came out a success.

Myth No. 5

"I don't need to build a presence to influence people. My clients already know me."

Bust it. NOW.

This is a lethal myth to bust, especially when you want to grow your business. Who doesn't want to get more clients? You might be doing well for yourself, but always remember that nothing is permanent. Business trends change, brand building trends change, and the client's needs change. Even the demands of your current clients change too! Nothing stays the same unless you close your business and don't do anything about it. You might be at whatever stage in your brand and business building, but you got to understand that you still need to make your presence felt by sharing the value that's free and easily available online. People need to know that you exist and that you care for the growth of your business and the quality of your presence; hence, you positively influence them to buy your service or product.

Myth No. 6

"If I give free content as value, they won't buy my service or product because I am already giving them so much."

Bust it. NOW.

Your free content is just the tip of the iceberg. You need to give them enough value for free that makes them aware of the subject or what can be done right away. But where the quality, depth, and actual action happens that is when they pay for your service or product. Free content is like a preview of what they will be experiencing when they consume your main content. If you want your audience to trust you, you have to help them get to know you before they plan to associate themselves with you. Your free content is the golden gate to your main product or service.

In the end, it is all about how you master the art of designing your presence as a powerful personal brand. You don't need to worry about factors and things that don't relate to the growth of your business.

A question for you to ponder on.

Which is more important?

Building a following and having thousands of people following you without really doing business with you?

Or

Building a presence that is evergreen and becomes a strong asset for your business to grow to a whole new level steadily and purposefully?

Your choice.

Do you need a coach? Find out here –

https://form.questionscout.com/60016d8d79cec37001f81de1

Write to me -

info@diyaasrani.com

Book a call directly –

https://calendly.com/diyaasrani/claritycallwithdiya

www.ingramcontent.com/pod-product-compliance
Lightning Source LLC
Chambersburg PA
CBHW030856180526
45163CB00004B/1601